'A useful collection of ideas and resources for promoting essential movement, play and physical activity in the early years.'

— Anne O'Connor, Co-Founder and Principal Consultant,
Primed for Life Training Associates

'This book is a call for embodied learning. Young children must use their bodies to learn well, and weaving physical activity and active play into everyday experiences across all elements of the curriculum to harness their great love of movement and action will reap great rewards for learners and teachers alike.'

— Jan White, Consultant for Outdoor Provision and
author of Every Child a Mover

LEARNING THROUGH MOVEMENT AND ACTIVE PLAY IN THE EARLY YEARS

of related interest

Yoga for Speech-Language Development
Susan E. Longtin and Jessica A. Fitzpatrick
Illustrated by Michelle Mozes
ISBN 978 1 84819 258 4
eISBN 978 0 85701 205 0

Sitting on a Chicken
The Best *Ever* 52 Yoga Games to Teach in Schools
Michael Chissick
Illustrated by Sarah Peacock
ISBN 978 1 84819 325 3
eISBN 978 0 85701 280 7

Go Yogi!
Everyday Yoga Asanas for Children
Emma Hughes
Illustrated by John Smisson
ISBN 978 1 84819 341 3
eISBN 978 0 85701 297 5

How to Get Kids Offline, Outdoors, and Connecting with Nature
200+ Creative activities to encourage self-esteem, mindfulness, and wellbeing
Bonnie Thomas
ISBN 978 1 84905 968 8
eISBN 978 0 85700 853 4

Inclusion, Play and Empathy
Neuroaffective Development in Children's Groups
Edited by Susan Hart
Foreword by Phyllis Booth
ISBN 978 1 78592 006 6
eISBN 978 1 78450 243 0

LEARNING THROUGH MOVEMENT AND ACTIVE PLAY IN THE EARLY YEARS

A Practical Resource for Professionals and Teachers

TANIA SWIFT

Jessica Kingsley *Publishers*
London and Philadelphia

First published in 2017
by Jessica Kingsley Publishers
73 Collier Street
London N1 9BE, UK
and
400 Market Street, Suite 400
Philadelphia, PA 19106, USA

www.jkp.com

Library of Congress Cataloging in Publication Data
A CIP catalog record for this book is available from the Library of Congress

British Library Cataloguing in Publication Data
A CIP catalogue record for this book is available from the British Library

ISBN 978 1 78592 085 1
eISBN 978 1 78450 346 8

Printed and bound in Great Britain

MIX
Paper from
responsible sources
FSC
www.fsc.org   FSC® C013604

CONTENTS

ACKNOWLEDGEMENTS

Thank you to Elizabeth Hutton for proof-reading, editing and literary advice.

Thank you to Melinda Swift and Nigel Robinson for your support through the process of writing the book.

Thank you to Naomi Molesworth, Helen Miles and Karl Rogerson for your knowledge, expertise and inspiration in the early days.

INTRODUCTION

A few years ago, I was delivering one of my training courses for teachers in England and, while explaining what children will learn from making and playing with a paper fortune teller in pairs – mathematics (shapes and numbers), language (writing on the fortune teller), communication (working in pairs), physical development (the 'forfeits' were physical movements) and I could go on and on – it suddenly dawned on me that I was not teaching them new, ground-breaking, mind-boggling ideas, I was teaching them what children have naturally done for generations. As children we just played with fortune tellers, climbed trees, cycled around every day (I am from South Africa and so probably could do more than those of you in countries that are not so blessed with sunny climes) and generally were outside most of the time playing.

In all honesty, irrespective of what country you are in, what curriculum you should adhere to, if any, the climate of the country or cultural beliefs they are brought up with, young children should be able to move and explore for a large part of each day. Movement and physical activity is part of being alive; it helps keep us healthy, contributes towards good mental health and creates opportunities to learn through experience, experiment and exploration.

As children spend more time indoors – in front of screens, being driven about and generally moving away from a natural lifestyle – and at the same time governments and decision makers place more and more value on academia and much less value on physical development and activity, we need to provide reasons and research to explain what we have been doing and what has worked for centuries.

This book will explore how movement and active play underpins and supports physical development, brain development, learning, social and emotional development and a positive attitude towards physical activity and learning.

There are many schools of thought about education and how children should learn; generally, however, people who professionally care for young children agree that play and physical activity is important for children. Furthermore, the impact of physical activity on brain development has become common knowledge for most professionals. However, it is one thing to know that something is good for children but another to know how to provide the best opportunities for development and learning in a mostly child-directed environment, supported by enjoyable planned sessions and lessons. We need to look at what has worked in the past and then build on this with the newfound knowledge that modern research and our own experiences have taught us.

Society values children's academic achievement and much pressure is placed on practitioners and parents to get children reading, writing and counting at a young age. Unfortunately, less importance is currently placed on children's physical development. In addition to the obvious effects we are seeing in the rise in childhood obesity, this somewhat blinkered view also has the potential to hamper cognitive development. Physical activity not only impacts on social skill development, language, communication, mathematics and self-esteem but children also develop their cognitive skills through play. Such unrealistic expectations are placed on children by governments and other policy makers that it can sometimes seem difficult to find the time to allow children to just naturally develop. It is therefore important to realise how much children are learning while playing, moving and taking part in planned physical education lessons.

SCHOOL READINESS

School readiness is when a child has reached a stage in their development where they are able to learn effectively. For a child to be school ready they need to have had many opportunities to play, explore, be active, discover their own abilities, be challenged and develop positive relationships with their peers. They will need to have developed in four areas:

1. physical, including motor development and health

2. emotional and social

3. cognitive

4. language.

If a child has not developed sufficiently by the time they start formal education they will struggle to sit at a desk, concentrate, write, cope emotionally, take part in physical activities and communicate, all of which can have a negative impact on their academic achievement, social engagement and experience of school life.

ENGAGING CHILDREN

The research and findings of neuroscience and of many theorists, such as Lev Vygotsky and Jean Piaget, into child learning and development show that children learn best when they are fully engaged.[1, 2, 3] When children are enjoying what they are doing, when they are being challenged within their capability, when they are exploring and experiencing new and different things and different environments, they will be fully engaged. Being fully engaged in this manner not only provides the best conditions for learning, but also helps to develop higher order thinking, which children will need to be able to achieve in school and later life.

When caring for young children we should therefore create an environment that enables and encourages them to explore and engage in new experiences (see Chapter 10 for more information). We also need to provide engaging activities that link to their changing interests and abilities, that are creative and engage their imagination, and that are repetitive but include small changes that challenge them.

WHY MOVEMENT AND ACTIVE PLAY?

A child sitting still is a child limiting their exploration, discovery and learning. When they are running around with their fellow superheroes, moving to music, jumping over a stream or building a den, they are learning. They are discovering what they can do, how they are similar and different to their peers, distances, how things

---

1   Fredricks, J.A., Blumenfeld, P.C. and Paris, A.H. (2004) 'School engagement; Potential of the concept, state of the evidence.' *Review of Educational Research 74*, 1, 59–109.

2   Immordino-Yang, M.H. and Damasio, A. (2007) 'We feel, therefore we learn: The relevance of affective and social neuroscience to education.' *Mind, Brain and Education 1*, 1, 3–10.

3   Willis, J. (2007) 'The Neuroscience of Joyful Education.' Available at www.scribd.com/document/290908986/The-Neuroscience-Joyful-Education-Judy-Willis-Md, accessed on 19 December 2016.

fit together, amounts of objects needed, how to communicate in a group, rhythm of language, and so much more.

Children will only do, and learn to do, what they want to do; if they find something boring, uninteresting or too challenging they may not engage and if they do, they may not learn much and may find it upsetting or stressful, meaning the whole experience could have a negative impact on the child's learning rather than having a positive outcome.

When young children play and are physically active, they are 'working': they are learning new skills, developing their brain and discovering the world around them. When children play they are discovering, collecting and gathering new information and ideas and applying this information. They are also developing and mastering new and old physical, mental, emotional and cognitive skills.

Active play is a combination of fine and gross motor activities that impacts children's physical health and development, their social and intellectual development and develops their brain. When children are partaking in active play, either through self-directed or adult-led activities, they will be engaged, learning and developing. Passive play, where children are not partaking in the activity but watching and learning from others does not provide the learning opportunities or experience that children need to develop fully, so get them moving and engaging.

Young children should be on the move most of the day. They should be pottering, where they will be discovering much about the world around them and also about what they can do. When not pottering or resting, they should be running, jumping, spinning and getting their heart rate up regularly during the day. Children should be moving in all types of ways, both in ways that they choose themselves and in ways that are led by adults, ensuring they develop all the skills they need. There are many skills children need to develop (see the early years physical skills section in Chapter 2: Physical Development), which should eventually lead to children becoming proficient at the fundamental movement skills. In order for children to develop, and eventually master, these skills they need regular instructional time and support from adults who care for them. This is where structured active play and physical activities are important for young children.

In order for a young child to grow and develop how and when they should, they need to be exposed to many hours a day of play, made up of free play and structured play.

Free or Self-directed Play

Free (or self-directed) play is when children are allowed the freedom to choose what they do and, if possible, where they do it. Adults are still able to have an impact on their experience of self-directed activities by providing an enriching environment, allowing children to spend time in the outdoors, offering challenges and asking questions about their achievements and intentions, which can be great teachable moments. Children will also be more likely to take chances and try new things if they feel safe and secure, which is usually due to the relationships they have with the adults caring for them and the confidence that has been instilled in them.

Structured Play or Activities

Self-directed play is important for children, but also providing structured activities will help children develop specific abilities and skills that they need as they grow older. Structured activities also allow for inclusive play and can introduce children to experiences they may not have tried on their own. It is important to take children's abilities and interests into account and build from what they can already do, making the activities more engaging, achievable and enjoyable.

Play helps children to:

- think creatively
- develop problem-solving skills
- develop language (though social interaction)
- develop social skills
- understand and learn about the world through real-world experience
- develop higher level thinking
- develop executive function skills and self-regulation.

EXECUTIVE FUNCTION SKILLS AND SELF-REGULATION

Executive function skills allow us to plan, organise and complete many tasks. It is incredibly important that we develop our executive functions when we are children as it will help us in many ways. Executive function skills allow us to control ourselves when becoming upset or angry or being faced with the unexpected, they allow us to be more flexible in our thinking, to plan priorities and work towards a goal or outcome, and enable us to switch from one activity or task to another.

In order for children to develop their executive function skills they need positive relationships with the adults who care for them, access to stimulating environments, creative play, physical exercise and social interactions, and we need to help them to develop coping mechanisms which enable them to deal with stress. Research has shown that self-directed play, rather than structured play, has a huge impact on the development of executive function skills.[4]

THE ADULT'S ROLE

How and what children learn is a three-way partnership between them, those who care for them outside the home and their parents. It is not *what* we or their parents teach them that provides the most valuable learning experiences, those experiences are gained through the environment we expose them to, the tools we provide that will excite and motivate them to want to learn, the experiences and opportunities their parents provide for them and how we work in partnership with their parents. It is important to focus on the process rather than the outcome and, by allowing children to explore and discover, we can lead them to many learning experiences motivated by awe and wonder, while they are moving, playing and being active, indoors and out.

As children get older and move into the more formal schooling systems around the world, many are forced into a standardised way of learning, even though they are all individuals, learn in different ways and have different interests. In the early years we are fortunate enough to be given the freedom to allow children to learn and

---

4   Frost, J.L. (1998) 'Neuroscience, play and child development.' Available at http://files.eric.ed.gov/fulltext/ED427845.pdf, accessed on 19 December 2016.

develop as individuals. However, the more we know about how to support their learning and development the more we can offer and provide to enhance their everyday experiences. We need to develop the knowledge, creativity and confidence that will allow us to provide exciting and effective learning experiences for the young children we care for, inspire, develop and teach.

There is a Finnish saying, 'Those things you learn without joy you will forget easily', which is reflected in their early years curriculum; children in Finland only start formal education at the age of seven. They have very little homework, children are not divided into sets based upon ability and the main daily activity for young children is play. However, since 2000 they have topped just about every educational league table for school standards! This is testament to the fact that young children do not need to sit still to learn. In fact, they need the opposite.

WHAT YOU WILL FIND IN THIS BOOK

The aim of this book is to equip those who work with young children with the knowledge, confidence and motivation to provide their children with the best learning experiences and outcomes that they can.

It will concentrate on two areas:

1. How movement underpins cognitive learning, brain development, social skills and the well-being of children.

2. Information, ideas, tools and tips for creating activities to help children learn through movement and being active.

It is divided into chapters that will address the areas of learning that are covered by most educational curriculums around the world, such as mathematics, language and literacy, and personal, social and emotional development. Each section will identify how physical activity can underpin children's learning and how activities can be used to enhance their learning. It will provide the reader with information and knowledge to help them develop their own practice, practical ideas for them to use on a day-to-day basis and case studies and examples of good practice from peers in the early childhood sector. Some information will be reiterated in different sections as a reminder of its importance.

This book is aimed at developing the knowledge and skills of those who care for and work with young children. The information in it is relevant for able-bodied children, children with disabilities and those with special educational needs, as its application is wide-ranging and accessible for all.

The book will explore:

- how physical activity and active play support learning in all areas

- how we can deliver activity sessions and physical education lessons as well as provide an environment that will enhance children's natural learning experiences, while not placing formal constraints on them

- good practice shared by other teachers and early years practitioners

- physical activity ideas to enhance children's learning

- the importance of taking regular unstructured activity breaks to enhance children's learning.

Information is provided in a manner that is accessible and easy to put into practice, as opposed to being academic observation. It is non-prescriptive, allowing it to be useful for an array of different circumstances and groups of children, such as a reception class of 30 children with mixed ability, including children with special needs, a nursery class with mild to moderate physical difficulties, groups of highly active children or a group of children who are reluctant to be active.

During the many years of working with children in nurseries, children's centres and schools, and supporting and training teachers and early years practitioners, I have developed activities that correspond with young children's needs and interests and that really impact their development and learning. I have shared some of these ideas in the final chapter of the book (Chapter 11), along with some old favourites. Chapters 3–8 include a list of the activities found in Chapter 11 that will support teaching of that particular area of learning. You can use these ideas exactly as they are or use them as a starting point and add your own flair to make them work for your children and you.

Chapter 1

THE IMPORTANCE OF MOVEMENT AND ACTIVE PLAY

The importance of physical activity is often only considered in the context of children staying 'healthy'. In fact, it is an incredibly effective learning tool for early years. When children are enjoying physical activities, they are achieving a lot more than simply moving: they are also learning to communicate with others, beginning to understand the subtle nuances of interacting with their peers, mathematical concepts, enriching their vocabulary and developing their brains.

Children's early years experiences impact their immediate and future health and well-being, laying the foundations for their future and shaping the adults that they will become. When babies are born their brains are not fully developed and, even though genes are intrinsic to the make-up of their brains, experiences in early years also play a large role, in particular those enriching experiences of which movement and active play make up a large proportion.

As the brain in young children is shaped by and responds to the environment, children learn through activities and enhancing experiences. Movement is therefore essential for babies', infants' and young children's brain development and their learning.

Children in early years education are fortunate as they do not have the same stringent constraints placed on them by government and educational bodies as older children do. We should therefore take full advantage of this opportunity and help children learn and develop in the way they do naturally – through movement, play and exploring the environment, supported by positive relationships.

As teachers, parents and carers, what do we want? We want children to grow, develop and flourish physically, socially, emotionally and academically. We therefore need to provide them with an enriching environment and opportunities to play in ways that will expand their knowledge and experience. Children are natural learners and if their curiosity is sparked they will want to learn. Whether you are five or 105 years old, if you find something enjoyable and interesting you are more likely to want to do more and will be more likely to learn from the experience.

Furthermore, it has become common knowledge that children, particularly young children, do not learn different subjects independently from each other, they learn mathematical concepts through puzzles, water play and scoring games, they develop their language and communication through active stories and rhymes, they discover how to interact with others socially when playing in pairs and groups and develop positive attitudes towards themselves through their achievements, such as catching a ball or building a structure. Even though there are ongoing discussions about how cross-curricular learning can impact a child's development and learning experience, we are still exploring how to best teach in this way. Children's physical, cognitive, emotional and social development do not happen independently of each other, so why would we expect these areas to be taught independently of each other?

Teachers and early years practitioners are also constantly looking for ideas and support to allow them to plan efficiently as more and more pressure is being placed on them to achieve results and do more paperwork. This often impacts negatively on the care and support they provide the children, as well as the children's learning and development outcomes. However, this desire to save time can have a positive outcome if it means taking a rounded view on all of a child's learning potential within a single task. We can see this when providing information and tools to help plan for learning through movement and play where those who work with young children will identify many more outcomes being achieved at the same time, rather than individually. Hence, when supporting children's learning through movement and active play we need to be aware of how movement and active play underpins cognitive learning, brain development, social skills and well-being, taking a holistic, rather than a single skill view of learning.

Society values children's academic achievement, and pressure is placed on practitioners and parents to get children reading, writing and counting at a young age. Unfortunately, this can negatively impact children's opportunities to be active and to play. This has the potential to hamper a child's academic achievement. Movement and active play are intrinsic to learning in the young and forcing them into more formal learning too soon can be counter-productive. When children in early years play, they are not just having fun; they are actually 'working' and are building vital skills in every developmental area.

THE BASICS

When caring for children, it makes sense to find out as much as you can about their past. Have they had much opportunity to be active? Do they have a garden? Did they crawl when they were babies? This will paint a picture of how they got to where they are now, especially for children who are behind in their physical and academic development. Often questions about transition arise; however, children should be supported through a process of natural progression rather than transition from one year to the next. Ultimately, it is about children developing and learning through play, movement and enjoyment. They are then more likely to develop the skills and abilities they require for more complex games and sports whilst being happy, feeling good about themselves and achieving academically.

There are many schemes of work, guidelines and resources available to support practitioners in their delivery of physical activities. These can all be really useful supportive tools; but it is just as important for teachers and practitioners to have the knowledge to underpin how these tools can best be used for the children in their care. With a little bit of knowledge, teachers and practitioners will be best placed to understand the needs of the children in their care. With that in mind, no play or activity should ever be considered 'wrong', unless a child is about to hurt themselves or others, and it is important to reinforce this with children.

It is important to encourage children to try moving in different ways in order for them to develop all the skill they need to move competently. Before children can become proficient in any skill, they need to develop the foundation abilities of balance, coordination and spatial awareness and, as they get older, master agility (the ABCS). These foundation abilities will greatly impact children's physical achievement so it is worth getting it right early on. Too often children are referred to occupational therapists or physiotherapists for developmental delays when all they actually need is a bit more time to explore the environment and catch up due to too little physical activity when they were younger. The ABCS are so important for young children as they underpin their physical development and ability as well as impact on academic achievement. The ABCS should therefore always remain in the forefront when planning and delivering physical activities with young children.

Note: there are certain conditions, such as dyspraxia, autism and cerebral palsy, which can inhibit a child's development of the ABCS. Irrespective of this, providing any child with as many opportunities as possible for movement and active play will have a huge impact on their development.

Agility

Agility is the speed with which a child performs a movement and the ability to change the direction of the body in an efficient and effective manner without losing their balance. In order to become agile, we require a combination of:

- static balance
- dynamic balance
- speed
- strength
- coordination
- spatial awareness.

Children in early years will first need to develop the above abilities through regular access to a variety of activities and free play before they develop agility.

WHY AGILITY IS IMPORTANT

Levels of agility will impact our athleticism and achievement in sport. Supporting the development of agility in children will make them more likely to participate in sport and encourage a life-long love of exercise, health and self-worth.

ACTIVITIES

Agility drills are not appropriate for young children. However, they will begin to develop agility and speed naturally if they have access to regular movement and play. Some activities that help develop agility in younger children include:

- jumping moves and other activities that promote spatial awareness

- relay races

- obstacle courses

- active stories

- stop and go.

Top Tip – First focus on supporting children to develop their balance, coordination and spatial awareness, and these foundation abilities will underpin higher levels of agility as they get older.

Balance

Balance is a learned ability that develops with experience. It is the ability to maintain and sustain a controlled body position when performing a task and is required for everything we do. Balance will impact a child's ability to perform locomotive skills and ball skills, as well as to perform everyday tasks such as dressing, reaching and even sitting upright on a chair. It is therefore important to include balance activities in children's daily activities.

There are four primary components of balancing:

- proprioception or spatial awareness – understanding the space around (and under) you and how it will affect your ability to balance

- vestibular system in the ear – controls your balance by monitoring the position of your head

- strength of the back and stomach muscles, hips and ankles – coordinate what movements are required in order to maintain balance

- visual system – allows you to see where your body and head are in relation to your surroundings and also sense any movement that may affect your balance.

Starting with simple exercises, for example, balancing in a place holding onto a chair, and moving in gradual steps to more complex balancing manoeuvres – such as balancing whilst moving and holding an object – is an approach that will support children to confidently develop their balance.

Balance can be divided into two categories: static and dynamic.

STATIC BALANCE

Static balance involves a stable centre of gravity, with the body being still and firm over the base, for example, standing on one foot or performing a headstand.

DYNAMIC BALANCE

Dynamic balance is maintaining control and balance while moving, for example, walking on a balancing beam, riding a bicycle, balancing while throwing or catching a ball.

- 3-year-old children should be able to walk along a wide balance board.

- 4-year-old children should be able to walk part way along a narrow beam.

- 5-year-old children should be able to walk the length of a narrow beam.

Top Tip – Try balancing on different body parts, not just your feet. Balance on hands and knees, then take one hand or one of your knees off the ground. Balance on your bottom or sideways on one hand and one foot.

SPECIAL NEEDS BALANCE

Bouncing children with special physical needs on a gym ball or on their parent's knee is an activity that will help them develop their balance. As you bounce them they will need to keep their balance. Depending on the level of support the child needs, hold them by their hands or their trunk. As with babies, place different cushions on the floor and encourage the child to crawl over them. Children will need to keep their balance as they tackle the different levels of surfaces.

Coordination

Coordination is intrinsic to everyday tasks and is developed in the early years through gross motor and fine motor activities. It does not come easily to all children, so we need to provide them with many opportunities to play, explore, create and be active.

HAND-EYE AND FOOT-EYE COORDINATION

This is the ability to guide the hand or foot movements with the eye, such as catching, striking or kicking a ball. Hand-eye coordination is also important for handwriting, reading and copying from a board or other surfaces.

BILATERAL COORDINATION

This is the ability to use both sides of the body at the same time in a controlled and organised manner. Bilateral coordination shows that both sides of the brain are communicating which allows our hands and feet to work together. Bilateral coordination is learnt in stages – first, using both sides of the body to do the same thing, for example, clapping; second, using one hand and holding the other still, for example, throwing a ball; and finally, alternating movements, for example, skipping, marching and crawling. Eventually children do different things on each side of the body, for example, writing or cutting with scissors with one hand and holding the paper with the other.

Bilateral coordination not only allows us to achieve gross motor actions such as running, skipping and star jumps but also allows us to do daily activities, such as writing, cutting with scissors, climbing stairs and cooking.

SWINGING

Swinging helps children to develop coordinated, practised movements as they swing. There are many movements that need to be coordinated to allow children to propel themselves forwards and backwards. It is easier for children to work out the movements than for adults to teach them, but you can support this development by standing in front of them and ask them to touch your hands with their feet.

SWIMMING

Children need to coordinate their arms, legs and much more in order to propel themselves forward without sinking. Swimming is great for developing coordination and is fantastic exercise and fun.

Top Tip – If you do not have regular access to a swimming pool, children can practise their strokes on the ground (on a soft surface). They can lie on their stomachs or backs and they should try to coordinate their kicking and arm strokes.

Ultimately, if a child does not develop good coordination, it will impact all areas of their life.

Spatial Awareness

Spatial awareness can be defined as the awareness of the body in space (how they fit into a space), and the child's relationship to objects in the space (how they fit into a space in relation to other objects or people).

Children will need to have adequate body awareness before they will be able to develop spatial awareness. It is therefore important for children to experience many body awareness activities when they are young. Once children understand how their bodies fit together they will then be able to form an understanding of the relationship their body has with other objects and people within a space.

The best way to support the natural development of spatial awareness and body awareness is to allow babies and children to explore the environment freely. However, there are various situations that might inhibit or prevent the natural development of spatial awareness, including conditions such as autism and cerebral palsy that impact on childen's perception, not receiving adequate opportunity to explore the environment freely from an early age and missing out on key developmental stages due to long-term illness.

Doing activities such as target games, body awareness activities and obstacle courses where children need to fit into a space will support the development of spatial awareness. The ideal scenario is to let them run free and explore the space around them. They might bump into others and objects but this is how they will learn.

As in all areas of physical activity, spatial awareness has a much wider application than purely large movement. For example, children use spatial awareness in mathematics and literacy to process and arrange information on the page and in their linguistic and cognitive development to sort and express left from right, up from down.

Older children who have spatial awareness difficulties may:

- be unsure of how to arrange information on a page

- struggle with structuring and organising written work

- have some visual perception difficulties

- appear clumsy and bump into objects and others when moving around

- have difficulty playing games, doing physical activities and using apparatus

- find mathematics difficult

- confuse positional language such as left, right, over, under, etc.

- struggle to follow directions that use positional language.

Activities that can help children to develop better spatial awareness include:

- target games, for example, throwing beanbags into objects or over a line or object to help develop better perspective of distance and size

- obstacle courses where children need to fit into spaces to help develop a better understanding of space and how they fit into it

- movement to music to develop the use of their body and isolation of body parts, use of space and avoiding others and other objects

- hopscotch to help develop balance and develop understanding of how they fit into spaces

- action songs using parts of the body to help develop body-awareness which is an important component of spatial awareness

- climbing large equipment or climbing frames to help develop an understanding of position in relation to objects, such as over, under, through, between and around

- instruction-based activities such as Simon Says and 'What's the Time, Mr Wolf?' to help develop body awareness and avoiding others and other objects.

However, do remember that the best way for young children to develop agility, balance, coordination and spatial awareness is to explore and play freely and develop naturally.

Top Tip – Unless the activity requires children to move in a circle, always encourage them to use the whole space. This will help them learn to avoid others moving in different directions. A good way to encourage this is to place markers or spots around the area and instruct children to move between the markers/spots.

DIFFERENTIATION AND PROGRESSION

Children will develop at their own pace and need to be given the space and opportunity to do so. When providing structured activities for young children, differentiation and progression at the right time can impact on how all children achieve and grow.

Activities such as active stories and movement to music provide differentiation naturally as children are able to engage at their own level. Note that if you are including more challenging tasks in these activities you will need to be aware of progressing with small steps to allow all to feel included.

Differentiation

In all planned lessons and sessions, it is important to plan for children with a variety of levels of ability. This will allow all children to push themselves and develop but will not make it too challenging, otherwise they will not enjoy the activity and will become demotivated. On the other hand, if the activity is not challenging enough, children may become bored and lose interest.

Progression

Children will progress at different rates, so it is important to plan for progression of all activities, tasks and skills. Repetition is important for young children, with regular small changes to allow for them to move forward developmentally.

Structured Sessions with Children of Different Abilities and with Special Educational Needs

Use activities that include various skills, starting with skills that all the children are able to do. Slowly progress children who are more physically advanced by adding more complex skills to the activity, while the less able children continue at the level that is appropriate for them.

Set up three or four activities in a large area. Ensure that at least one of the activities is suitable for all children in the group. More advanced children can rotate through all activities during the lesson while the less able children can remain at the activity or activities that are appropriate for their ability level.

Differentation and progression with PATTER

P PEOPLE
How will changing the people change this (individual, pairs, groups, etc.)?

A ACTIVITY / MOVEMENT
How can I change what is happening?

T TIMING
Would performing the task faster or slower change it?

T TASK
In what way can I change what they are doing?

E ENVIRONMENT / SPACE
How is the environment affecting this (large, small space, inside, outside, etc.)?

R RESOURCE / EQUIPMENT
Can we change what we are using to change this?

PATTER

Patter is a simple tool to help make small changes to activities and tasks, allowing for differentiation and/or progression. It can be used when planning or on an impromptu basis during activities. Having ideas to allow for differentiation before an activity will prepare you for when and if any changes are needed for inclusion of various levels of ability.

PHYSICAL ACTIVITY AND BRAIN DEVELOPMENT

When babies are born, their brains are not fully developed. Genes are intrinsic to the make-up of our brains; however, we must remember that enriching experiences in the early years, such as being active and developing positive relationships, also play a large role in how the brain develops. The formation of the young brain is influenced by experience and the environment, which can impact on it negatively and positively.

Scientific research has found that the brain has 'windows of opportunity' in the early years, where specific areas develop to their optimum at specific times from birth to around the age of 10 years. Most of us are not scientists so it is impossible to know when these 'windows of opportunity' occur; therefore, it is very important to provide young children with many opportunities to be active and also ensure that they are exposed to a wide variety of activities. If these 'windows of opportunity' are passed it is still possible to develop those particular areas of the brain, but the opportunity to develop them to their optimum may be missed. An example of this is the specific window for language acquisition, which starts to close at the age of five years. During this window of opportunity, children will only require exposure to the language in order to easily learn it and will speak without a foreign accent and they can also learn many languages simultaneously.

The brain's ability to change as we learn is known as 'plasticity', which occurs throughout our lives but most notably in the early years. Genes provide the blueprint for brains, but as children are exposed to experiences and environmental factors, the brain changes. Many environmental factors can impact on who we are and who we become. Research shows that some of the factors affecting our brains before birth and as young children grow, are attachment (positive or negative attachments), nutrition, sensory stimulation, motor stimulation, social exposure and experiences, as well as drugs and alcohol. Young brains are most vulnerable to these harmful factors but also have a higher capacity for recovery; as we get older it becomes harder to change our brain circuitry.

From birth until the age of three, children's brains grow and change at an almost unbelievable rate. Synapses – developed by neurons in order to join them to other neurons and to transmit information from one to the other – are formed faster during this period than at any other time in our lives. This is a process known as blooming. By age three we will have more synapses than we need, up to twice as many as in the adult brain. This is when a process called synaptic pruning takes place, where weaker or little used synapses are eliminated. Blooming and pruning are important to allow the brain to transmit efficiently, expanding its capacity to retain knowledge and develop to its optimum. This process continues until around the age of 10 years, so it is important for children's brain development for them to continue to have positive learning experiences, positive relationships and exposure to positive environmental factors.

PLANNING YOUR PHYSICAL ACTIVITIES

As young children's brains constantly tell them to move and fidget, it is difficult for them to sit still for too long. Rather than enforcing a static environment, it makes far more sense for us to tap in to this natural energy and allow children to learn through moving and exploring. We therefore need to ensure that physical activity is embedded in all areas of learning. Physical activity can be the underpinning link that supports all areas of development and subjects, considering activities that cover literacy, mathematics, social and emotional well-being and knowledge and, of course, understanding of the world.

Top Tip – When planning for all areas of learning, identify what you would like children to learn and then think about how you can help enhance their learning through a physical activity. This can be easily achieved by including a physical activity section in all your planning.

USE OF MUSIC, STORIES AND SONGS

Children respond to and enjoy music, singing, actions and stories. They love to move to the music, repeat rhymes and songs, and stories stimulate their imagination and help them to make sense of the world. As children are also predisposed to being active, making stories, songs and rhymes active adds another level of learning and enjoyment to these activities. Rather than expecting children to be seated and still when reading to them or singing a song, they will be experiencing what they are singing about, or discovering the world and characters within the story if acting them out. They will be the Grand Old Duke of York marching up that hill, the monkeys climbing the trees in the forest or feeling the effects of wind, sun, rain and snow.

OUTDOOR LEARNING

Research – and a growing body of evidence – shows that outdoor learning has a profound impact on children's emotional health, as well as their achievement at school. However, you do not need to be a scientist to appreciate all the benefits of children's outdoor experiences.

In order for young children to develop appropriately physically, emotionally and cognitively, as well as to develop neuro-motor maturity (when the brain integrates the senses of vision, hearing and motion), which is seen as a measure for school readiness, children need many experiences indoors, but even more so in the outdoors. To enable this to happen, children should be able to:

Build	Leap	Roll
Carry	Move fast	Run
Catch	Move slow	Slide
Climb	Pull	Swing
Hang	Push	Spin
Jump	Rock	Throw

Movement and active play in the early years is crucial for academic achievement, physical health, emotional well-being and social success throughout our lives. The following chapters will explore how movement and active play impacts the whole child in greater detail and the significant role you, as the adult, will play in the lives of children you care for.

Chapter 2

PHYSICAL DEVELOPMENT

Children need time to play and move on their own, discovering and exploring what their bodies can do. They also need adult-led activities that will challenge and guide them to develop to the best of their ability. They should be able to explore the environment and choose what they do for a large part of their day, developing skills naturally, and well-planned adult-led activities will enhance this development. These activities should be interesting for children in order for them to want to engage as well as instilling a love of being active.

Children also, of course, need to develop their fine motor skills. First, they need to develop many gross motor skills that underpin their fine motor ability and ability to approach tasks such as writing and cutting with scissors with dexterity. Consider the important components for effective writing: posture and balance for hand and arm control; strong muscles in their back, stomach, neck and shoulders to support refined hand and finger skills; bilateral co-ordination, for example using both hands at the same time; spatial awareness to organise what is on the page; and hand-eye coordination to guide their hand across the page. These are all developed through play and physical activities when children are young.

More and more children are lacking access to opportunities to be active and to develop appropriately at home, so we need to look at ways to support this development and encourage more positive activity.

HOW PHYSICAL ACTIVITY SUPPORTS CHILDREN'S PHYSICAL DEVELOPMENT AND WELL-BEING

It is essential for children to be on the move for a large part of each day in order for them to develop physically; through enjoyable activities they can learn about and come to understand the importance of taking care of themselves. Physical activity:

- develops gross motor and fine motor skills
- supports healthy growth and development
- develops and maintains flexibility
- develops decision-making and problem-solving skills
- supports brain development
- helps concentration
- promotes confidence and self-esteem
- helps children to learn about their bodies
- promotes resilience and helps children understand their abilities and boundaries
- helps children to learn about a healthy lifestyle and what is good for them
- enables children to learn about healthy food through food growing and food-based games and activities
- can teach hygiene through fun activities and active stories and rhymes
- supports the development of fine motor skills, communication skills and understanding, to allow for independent self-care or with a little support from others
- develops communication skills to allow children to share their feelings and to inform others of their needs.

Top Tip – If a child struggles to sit still and focus, include fine motor activities within gross motor activities to help them develop their fine motor skills whilst moving and playing. There is an array of activities that can be energetic as well as incorporating actions that use and develop children's fine motor skills. Some suggestions include picking up small buttons or stones during an active story, pretending they are treasure or the buttons of your suit. Peg racing games, where you have two 'washing' lines a few meters apart and children race to see how quickly they can unpeg the pegs from one line and peg them on the other line. You can also include digging for treasure in the sand in an outdoor obstacle course, and gestures with fingers and hands during movement to music and action songs.

HOW MUCH ACTIVITY?

Many countries around the world have developed physical activity guidelines; worryingly, many have not. Countries that are leaders in early years physical development and well-being include the United Kingdom, Australia, Canada, New Zealand and Finland. These countries recommend a variety of guidelines with regard to the amount of physical activity young children should be encouraged to do.

United Kingdom

The British Heart Foundation recommends that children from walking to five years old should be active for a minimum of 180 minutes a day to stay healthy and to develop. This needs to be spread out throughout the day and be a combination of moderate and high impact physical activities.

Moderate physical activity is when a child is moving their belly button from one place to another, for example pottering. This is called translocation of the trunk. High impact physical activity is when children have the opportunity to get their heart rate up or get out of breath.

Australia

Guidelines are similar, to those in the United Kingdom: children from birth to five should be physically active every day for at least three hours, spread throughout the day.

Children aged 5–12 years should be physically active for at least 60 minutes a day, including moderate to vigorous intensity physical activity.

Canada

Canadian guidelines also suggest that children aged 1–4 should be physically active every day for at least three hours, spread throughout the day. They should progress towards at least 60 minutes of high impact activity by five years of age.

New Zealand

There are no specific guidelines for children under the age of five, however they should be encouraged to move every day. Children and young people aged 5–18 years should be physically active for at least 60 minutes a day, including moderate to vigorous intensity physical activity.

Finland

Children up to the age of seven years should have at least two hours of brisk physical activity every day. Children and young people aged 7–18 years should be physically active for at least one to two hours a day, in a variety of age-suitable ways.

SKILLS

Early Years Physical Skills

There are many schemes of work and resources available for early years practitioners to follow; however, it is important to start with the basics and to provide activities that work for the children in your care. Practitioners need to be aware of the skills that children in early years need to develop and then help them to do so.

There are basic physical skills that children in early years need to learn. Teachers and early years practitioners will be aware of the obvious skills such as jumping, throwing, catching and balancing. There is an array of skills (listed later in this chapter) that children should have the opportunity to develop but are not receiving the opportunity to do so. Children also need to learn social and emotional skills such as taking turns, working in pairs and following rules through physical activities (see Chapter 5 for details).

Knowledge of skills is gained through education and supportive resources but also through experience. If a whole group of three year olds can jump and one cannot, then it will be obvious that that particular child will require additional support for that skill. But if you do not first focus on that basic skill there is a risk that you might take it for granted that all children can jump.

The outdoor and indoor environment can be set up to encourage children to try various skills by themselves. It is also important to give them opportunities to develop these skills more formally to ensure all children are developing appropriately. Furthermore, being able to do what their peers can do will have a marked impact on their confidence.

Top Tip – Repeat activities from your physical education lessons during the rest of the week to allow children to develop, explore and master specific skills and movements.

If a child is behind the other children developmentally in their year group or struggling with a specific skill, try to break down what they are attempting to do in order to identify why they are finding a specific skill challenging. Ask yourself questions such as is it a lack of balance, poor coordination or do they have poor muscular strength? Once you understand their needs, you can then better support them to achieve those skills. It is important that young children have many opportunities to repeat a skill with small challenges added from time to time. If the task is not achievable they may just give up.

When planning, identifying three or four skills a week and planning daily activities based on these skills will give activities more of a focus and ensure that children will have the opportunity to develop all the skills they need. The skills can be incorporated into known activities, used individually for simple activities throughout the week, used to create wild and wonderful active stories (they don't have to be best sellers!) and used to make up new games and activities based on a combination of skills.

Physical skills that children in the early years need to develop include:

Aiming	Evading	Pinching	Spinning
Avoiding	Experimenting	Pivoting	Splashing
Balancing	Galloping	Placing	Squatting
Bending	Gesturing	Pointing	Squeezing
Bouncing	Grasping	Predicting	Stacking
Carrying	Handling	Pressing	Standing
Catching	Hanging	Prodding	Stepping
Changing direction	Hiding	Pulling	Stopping
	Hitting	Pushing	Stretching
Chasing	Holding	Reaching	Striking
Clapping	Hopping	Rhythm	Taking
Climbing	Jumping	Rocking	Tiptoeing
Collecting	Kicking	Rolling	Tapping
Combining movements	Landing	Rotating	Throwing
	Leaping	Running	Touching
Crawling	Lifting	Scoring	Turning
Creeping	Lying	Shooting	Twisting
Cutting	Marching	Shuffling	Volleying
Digging	Matching	Skipping	Walking
Dodging	Painting	Sliding	Waving
Drawing	Picking up	Slithering	Wiggling
Dribbling		Speed	Writing

Fundamental Movement Skills

The next step for children is to develop control over the fundamental movement skills. The three categories of fundamental movement skills are body management skills, locomotor skills and object control skills. Children need to become proficient in fundamental movement skills in order to take part in more complex games and sport when they are older. If children do not have enough opportunity to practise these skills, then they could spend the rest of their lives playing catching up.

The fundamental movement skills are divided into three categories:

Body Management	Locomotor	Object Control
Balance	Crawling	Bouncing
Bending	Dodging	Catching
Climbing	Galloping	Dribbling
Jumping	Hopping	Kicking
Landing	Jumping for distance	Rolling
Leaping	Jumping for height	Striking
Rolling	Leaping	Throwing
Stopping	Running	
Stretching	Skipping	
Swinging	Walking	
Turning		
Twisting		

When teaching these skills, you should keep the following points in mind.

- It is important that children start to develop the fundamental movement skills in the early years of school.

- Children need instructional time to develop fundamental movement skills, as they do not necessarily come naturally.

- They need between 240 and 600 minutes of instructional time to become proficient in any one fundamental movement skill.

- Each skill should be focused on individually, or two or three skills at any one time.

Incorporating Skills into Known Activities

Not all exciting new activities need to be created from scratch, just add new layers to activities children already know. There is a reason why some games and activities have been around 'forever' – they work. So let us use what works and possibly even make it better! Here are some ideas.

TRAFFIC LIGHT GAME

Add new colours and link them to the skills of the week. Yellow could mean they should skip over the zebra crossing or pink could mean they should leap over the speed bumps.

SIMON SAYS

Incorporate the skills of the week into Simon Says to give the game more of a focus. Simon Says can also be used to create a body awareness activity, which is really important. If children are unaware of how their bodies fit together then they will struggle with spatial awareness.

ACTIVE STORIES

Active stories can be based on:

- animals – in the wild or a zoo
- everyday activities – cleaning the house or going shopping
- adventures – pirates or going to the moon
- fantasy – fairies, princesses and dragons
- the weather – different seasons or different types of weather
- stories you already know from books you read.

Incorporate any move or skills into your stories as in the examples below.

Jungle Adventure

You could bend under branches, wriggle out of brambles, jump over streams, gallop up the hill, roll down the hill, stretch up to reach for the monkeys, leap from stepping stone to stepping stone in the river, jump out of the water and then creep through the bushes.

Weather

You could spin like the wind, bend down and stretch up with your fingers wiggling when it rains, jump up and down like thunder, squat down and straighten up whilst moving arms in big circles in front of you when the sun is shining, freeze when it snows (standing still helps develop balance).

Child-led

You can also create stories with help and suggestions from the children. Ask them questions such as: What animal shall we be today? e.g. tiger; Where do we live? e.g. jungle; What do we like to do? e.g. climb trees, run up the hill; What do we eat? e.g. roast chicken, steak, grass.

Encourage children to think about how they have been moving that week (the skills) and to think how the moves would fit into the story. This might be too complicated for some children in which case a bit of guidance would be helpful.

Now Dance!

Once you have created and acted out a story you can create a dance to go with it. Ask children to help you identify music that matches the story and then to create moves to go with the music. Incorporate the skills of the week into the dance.

This is great for gross motor development. It can be done inside or outside and should be very energetic.

Active stories and games build motor skills while encouraging children's imagination, creativity and language skills. The stories are ideal for children of all ages and useful for when you care for a group with a variety of abilities or ages.

Creating New Activities

OBSTACLE COURSES

You can include almost any activity in an obstacle course, using the equipment you have and incorporating the skills you're working on at the moment.

Some examples include:

- jumping, hopping or leaping from spot to spot

- bending down to pick up a ball

- rolling a ball between two cones

- creeping and crawling through a box or tunnel

- pencil rolling along a mat.

Add a fine motor aspect into your obstacle courses, such as threading beads or using large tweezers to move fluffy balls from one container to another. This will help children who find it difficult to sit down and focus on fine motor activities.

ACTIVE CUBE

Equipment

Active Cube (with clear pockets); cards with skills and cards with numbers.

Numbers and Moves

- Place a different movement behind a number in each pocket (such as skip, hop, wiggle, etc.).

- Throw the cube.

- All children to say the number that is face up.

- Pull the movement card out.

- All children to say the movement that is face up.

- Do the movement the amount of times dictated by the number card.

This activity links with mathematics and literacy, and can also be played with animal cards. Identify animals that move in ways you would like the children to move that week.

MOVEMENT TO MUSIC

Select music that changes tempo such as a favourite nursery rhyme or classical music and encourage children to move to the tempo and levels (faster with faster tempo, reaching high if music is loud or high pitched and low if music is soft or low pitched).

Once children have grasped the concept of moving to the music add in skills, for example:

- skip when a particular sound is made, and wiggle when a different sound is made

- skip faster or slower depending on the tempo.

SELF-CARE

An important aspect of children's development is learning about being healthy and how to take care of themselves. This includes hygiene, toilet activities, hand-washing, dressing and undressing, healthy eating, hydration, physical activity and understanding how to lead a healthy life.

- Children need to learn about why physical activity is important for them and what it does for their bodies.

- Children need to learn about healthy eating and food growing. Much of this can be done through enjoyable activities.

- Children need to learn about wearing appropriate clothing for various weather, such as hats and sunscreen for protection, wellington boots and raincoats for rainy weather, etc.

- Children need to learn about the importance of hand-washing. Playing fun games and active stories or rhymes can help children to understand this.

- Find strategies to help children learn to dress and undress independently, such as pairing up children to help each other, help with part of the dressing and undressing and allow children to complete various aspects, such as leave one button for them, hook the zipper and allow the child to pull the zip up, etc.

- Help children who are struggling with self-care by leaving a last small step for them to complete, e.g. pulling up their trousers from just below the waist.

Top Tip – Active songs, active rhymes and active stories are a great way to teach children self-care. See the 'Use of Music, Stories and Songs' section in this chapter and ideas in Chapter 11 for more information.

Top Tip – Discussions with children before, during and after energetic exercises about the changes in their bodies and the effects of being active will help them to learn about their bodies and themselves.

BABY STEPS

The younger the child, the more repetition they will need in order to learn something new and the slower and smaller their progress will be. This can be challenging for practitioners who are new to early years and those who have been working in this area for a long time alike. Keep activities simple, repeat over and over again and make small changes or additions to the activity when you feel children are ready to progress.

IMAGINATION

Research has shown that habits formed in early years are more likely to continue when we are older, hence it is important to encourage young children to enjoy being physically active.[1] Most children love being active; however, more and more children are becoming reluctant to being active or to engage in high impact physical activity. This is due to environmental influences such as technology and being 'wrapped up in cotton wool' by their parents. We therefore need to find ways to encourage all to engage and enjoy. Incredibly useful tools in early years are imagination and active stories.

Create active stories using children's interests or their favourite stories, allow them to become characters in the story and give some or all children the responsibility of helping to develop the story. Active stories can be part of a PE lesson or anytime outside on an impromptu basis. They can be all about encouraging children to move or have specific skills as a focus (leap over a stream, bend under the branches, wriggle out of the brambles, etc.). They can also be used to teach children about feelings, about the world, healthy eating, taking care of themselves and many more important topics.

Always remember that if a child in early years is not engaged in an activity they will generally become miserable and 'misbehave',

---

1   Ouellette, J.A. and Wood, W. (1998) 'Habit and intention in everyday life: The multiple processes by which past behavior predicts future behavior.' *Psychological Bulletin 124*, 1, 54–74.

become bored and misbehave or find another way to entertain themselves and misbehave. Is this their fault?

If teachers and early years practitioners do not understand the basics of child physical development then the opportunity to build on this key area of learning will be missed and we will be letting our children down from the onset.

Shared Practice

Aesthetic Movement: Dance / Gym

By Alison Blomfield

I have taught physical education for 30 years and am at present Head of Prep Physical Education at St Francis College, Letchworth, a boarding school for girls aged 3–18 years old. As a direct result of one of Tania's CPD courses, I use her Mini Yo! cards to teach yoga postures to the Early Years Foundation Stage (EYFS) and Key Stage 1 (KS1) girls. I introduced yoga in to the PE Curriculum three years ago because I was seeing an increase in children with learning difficulties and a decline in pupils' core strength, which was impacting on their coordination, agility and flexibility. Babies spend more time in car seats these days and the use of tablets to entertain young children and sugary food and drink is impacting negatively on their development.

So rather than separate dance and gymnastic activities in the early years, I combine yoga, gym and dance as an aesthetic activity; I also do this with KS1 and 2. I teach the fundamental yoga postures, these form 'balances' in gym and movement for dances as pupils grow through later years. There are so many postures that can transfer across activities. Lotus is a beautiful calming pose and great for helping the children to sit still. Warrior pose transfers to throwing in athletics, sprint starts, or can be thought of as a defence pose in games. Pupils develop sequences or 'stories', using the postures taught, as well as any others they wish to bring to the lesson themselves. With EYFS and KS1 pupils, for example, I might tell a story and every time the yoga posture is mentioned in the story the pupils perform it.

If we take Tree pose, for example, I use it to help the children to create dances with trees as the theme. We go outside and observe trees, how weather or the seasons affect them. In November, dances will revolve around autumn and leaves, their colour and how the wind makes them swirl and twirl or squirrels scurrying up, down, around trees to find nuts. I encourage pupils to use Mini Yo! cards to make up their own story or sequence. Cross-curricular themes here are science, English (literacy) and art but I also include mathematics, history or any other subject within my lessons wherever it feels appropriate. For example, in gym we might count how many Tree rolls (Log rolls) it takes to go from one end of the mat to the other and then ask how many that would be over two mats.

Focusing on Lotus and Tree posture this week in the early lessons of my schemes, for example, as well as combining these with a few other basic postures, merely standing up in Tree then sitting down in Lotus whilst keeping one's hands above one's head is very good for strengthening the core and muscle conditioning. Not just for young children either!

The beauty of a yoga based physical education curriculum is that it covers all areas of learning and provides equal access to the curriculum for all, as well as keeping a calm yet productive classroom.

Personal, Social and Emotional Development

Yoga can help children to develop a sense of themselves, social skills and respect for others and a positive disposition to learn. It supports children's emotional well-being and helps them to understand and manage their feelings and behaviour.

Physical Development

Yoga helps children to use their senses and bodies to explore the world around them and make connections between new and existing knowledge. It gives them opportunities to be active and interact with nature or equipment indoors to improve their skills of coordination, control, manipulation and movement. It can help them to develop an understanding of a healthy lifestyle.

Communication and Language

Yoga is excellent for developing language, speaking and listening skills. Pupils can talk about what they see and how they are moving to show language in a wide range of situations.

Literacy

Yoga can help with learning the skills needed for reading and writing by using picture cards of poses and looking at the words as well as using their hands expressively to perform poses.

Mathematics

Yoga can help children to develop their understanding of numbers, calculating, shapes, space and measures. The group can stand in Tree in a circle, square or triangle, for example. Talk about the shape made, counting the number that make the shape, or the number on each side of the shape.

Understanding the World

Yoga can develop the knowledge, skills and understanding to help children make sense of their world. They can explore creatures, people, plants and objects to stimulate movement patterns and poses.

Expressive Arts and Design

Yoga can support children in developing their creativity by providing them with opportunities to express themselves and use their imagination. Talking about their performances encourages them to say how they feel, how an animal, plant or weather makes them feel and to share their ideas with the group.

Chapter 3

MATHEMATICS AND NUMERACY

When teaching mathematics to young children we often overcomplicate how we go about it. Mathematics is part of movement, play, exploration and creativity. Children will learn about mathematics and use mathematical concepts on a daily basis. It is an adult's role to help them understand these concepts, learn the mathematical vocabulary and develop an excitement about numbers.

Children discover mathematical concepts all around them as they play and explore. They will experience and learn about a variety of numbers, shapes, sizes, weights, heights and distances through activities such as role play, movement to music, exploring the outdoor environment and playing in mud.

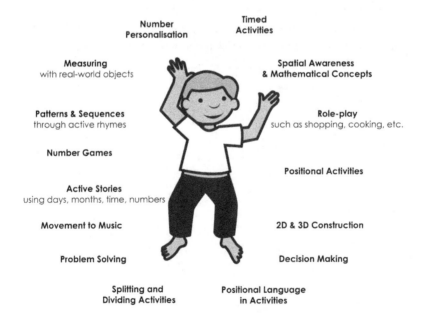

Number
Personalisation

Timed
Activities

Measuring
with real-world objects

Spatial Awareness
& Mathematical Concepts

Patterns & Sequences
through active rhymes

Role-play
such as shopping, cooking, etc.

Number Games

Positional Activities

Active Stories
using days, months, time, numbers

Movement to Music

2D & 3D Construction

Problem Solving

Decision Making

Splitting and
Dividing Activities

Positional Language
in Activities

HOW PHYSICAL ACTIVITY SUPPORTS CHILDREN TO LEARN MATHEMATICS AND NUMERACY

- Use of positional language in play, movement and physical education helps children to understand many mathematical concepts.

- Many activities develop decision-making and problem-solving skills.

- Children can develop a deeper understanding of mathematical concepts through use of shapes, measurements, distances, volume, etc. when they are playing.

- Young children need to develop spatial awareness to support mathematical development (see more details later in the chapter).

NUMBERS

Young children start to learn about numbers, how they fit together in sequences, counting, adding, subtracting, etc. They can learn to count by rote, but the numbers and sequences will have very little meaning. Create activities that allow children to make sense of numbers and how they are used, help them to understand how to use them in real-world situations.

- Action rhymes with or without numbers help children to understand patterns and sequencing.

- Active stories about days, months, seasons, etc. can help children make sense of time.

- Timed activities can help children to understand time (which is a difficult concept for young children).

- Active stories including numbers help children to make sense of numbers by putting them into context.

- Number games can help children to understand sequences of numbers to make sense of mathematical statements and language.

- Quantity games and matching groups or objects and people with the same and different quantities (more, fewer, half, quarter, equal parts, etc.) provide a 'real-world' opportunity to learn which will make more sense to young children.

- Splitting or dividing objects or groups of people into smaller parts teaches multiplication, division, size and groups.

- Counting games and keeping score are an effective way to make sense of sequencing and addition/subtraction.

- Personalisation of numbers through games, e.g. how many girls in the group or jump into the hula hoop if you are four, are a great way to teach numbers.

- Role play, including money handled at a shop, cooking and counting, etc., will put numbers into a real-world context, making more sense for children.

SHAPE, SPACE, MEASURE, GEOMETRY

Spatial awareness helps children to understand how shapes fit together. Children learn about themselves and the space around them through games and play.

- Playing games with shapes and different shaped objects helps children to work out how things fit and do not fit together.

- Movement to music, where different sounds indicate different movements, such as stomp like a heavy elephant, tiptoe like a light fairy, be as tall as a giant or, be as small as a mouse, will help children to understand height and weight.

- It is easier for children to start measuring with their own hands and using 'real-world' objects such as sticks, socks, shoes, pencils as measurement tools. This will make more sense to them than using rulers or tape-measures and will be more interesting and enjoyable.

- Activities and practical experience, be it in continuous provision or in adult-led activities, help children to understand mathematical language and concepts.

- Building and construction activities will require problem-solving, understanding of shapes, sizes, height, space, etc.

- Many activities will require the comparison of lengths and measures (height, volume, length, weight and overall size).

- Using various objects, substances and materials to build will allow children to explore and develop an understanding of the difference between types of shapes, including solid (3D) and flat (2D) shapes.

- Many games, activities and movements to music will teach children about positional language, such as forward, backward, sideways, zigzag and whole, half-, quarter- and three-quarter turns.

- When children are building structures they need to understand how objects fit together, numbers of objects needed, height of objects, etc.

Activities such as stacking, sorting and water play not only support fine motor development but also help children to understand mathematical concepts. When we teach children in early years to count they are generally learning 'parrot fashion'. This may present little real meaning to the child; however, calculating how objects fit together and playing games where they need to solve problems will better prepare them for mathematics. Open-ended activities provide more opportunity for children to apply their mathematical skills and knowledge, so provide many opportunities for children to create, build and use their imagination. They will also be faced with more challenges, stimulating a higher level of thinking.

Teaching a child to count with no real-world context may be good for the development of their mathematical language, but it is likely that the symbols will mean very little to them. Often when children are counting they leave a number out or do not count in sequence; this is because they learnt by rote and do not understand the meaning of these numbers.

According to the mathematician Keith Devlin, mathematics is more than just numbers, it is all about the world we live in and our lives; it is about being creative and is anything but dull, as so many people see it.[1] This becomes apparent when you see how children learn about shapes, sequencing, measures and even numbers when playing and exploring.

---

1 Devlin, K. (1993) *The Language of Mathematics*. London: Palgrave Macmillan.

NATURAL DEVELOPMENT

Examples of how children will learn mathematics through self-directed movement and active play in the early years include:

- building a den, which involves having to figure out what size it needs to be, the measurements of the structure, how many sides it has and the height. They also need to try to understand how many children are in the group and how big the den needs to be so they can all fit

- making mud pies and using different shaped and sized containers to create different pies

- working out the height of themselves and length of objects by lying down and placing sticks, or other objects alongside them

- packing away resources and toys before lunch and having to sort and identify what belongs where

- moving in, out, over, under and around the climbing structure which helps them to develop spatial awareness. It also helps them to understand distance, direction and ultimately how things fit together around them

- baking, which involves having to weigh some ingredients and using measuring containers for some ingredients, as well as counting out numbers of other ingredients

- constructing towers and bridges out of cardboard boxes and other material available in the environment

- learning number sequences when playing with and sorting toys such as cars, blocks, balls and plastic bricks

- using objects such as stacking cups with varying sizes to teach them about weight and dimension

- growing food, which helps children to learn about time and the life cycle of plants. They can measure their plants, compare size, height and growth (which plant is growing fastest and which is growing slowest?). Children can also learn sequencing through plant growing, such as which was planted first, which was planted today, do you remember what we picked yesterday and which ones should be pick tomorrow, what do we need to do before we plant and after we plant?

- playing with water, mud, sand, gravel and stones to create different shapes, add, divide, and make marks
- climbing trees and other climbing structures which involves problem-solving and using positional abilities.

Learning mathematics through activities provided by adults in the early years can include:

- exploring height and weight through movement to music, e.g. stomp, tiptoe, high, low
- learning about patterns from active nursery rhymes, including repetition and sequences
- using large die to identify how many times to jump, how many steps to take and how far we need to hop
- keeping score during competitive and cooperative games
- obstacle courses, e.g. fitting into spaces, number of times to do a task, height, position
- adults role-modelling mathematical language and creating mathematical discussions
- problem-solving to achieve a task.

It would be very difficult, if not impossible, to develop our mathematical thinking and understanding without creativity. We need to explore, try new things and experiment to develop these important skills. When children are being active and playing they are at their most creative, which makes it a perfect time for them to explore and develop these skills. Learning through real-world experiences will help children understand and develop this knowledge and without this practical application it will quickly be forgotten. As with all other areas of development, the more relevant and engaging you can make a topic, skill or activity, the greater the chance that the skill will be developed and used in the correct way in the future.

THE ADULTS' ROLE

It is important that teachers, early years practitioners, parents and carers understand the foundations of mathematics. Although children learn mathematical concepts naturally, they will still rely on the adults who care for them to enhance their learning and teach them mathematical language and concepts.

Ways we can support young children to learn mathematics include creating a mathematically rich environment, being aware of teachable moments and, above all, making mathematics enjoyable, creative and engaging. Young children learn through repetition, so think about what mathematical activities work indoors and whether they can be repeated outdoors, making them bigger and possibly messier.

Share positive attitudes towards learning mathematics; be aware of teachable moments which allow you to ask questions about what children are doing. This questioning will stimulate their higher order thinking and problem-solving and increasing your understanding of how you can effectively teach them in a cooperative manner during child-initiated play and when leading planned activities. A teacher needs to become a learner, so show curiosity, question, listen and learn – this will model problem-solving and being a cooperative learner.

Top Tip – Creating fun mathematics activities will create positive attitudes towards this area of learning, children really should not be sitting down to learn about size, amounts, shapes, distances.

Mathematical Language and Vocabulary

Teaching children mathematical vocabulary such as counting, bigger, smaller, higher and keeping score can happen during many activities. For example:

- Let's stomp like an elephant and now walk on our tiptoes like giraffes. Which animal do you think is taller? Which animal do you think is wider?

- Can you throw your beanbag into the hoop that is furthest away from you?

- How many groups have you been split into? How many are in each group?

Engaging them in mathematical conversation anytime, anywhere will broaden their mathematical language. Asking questions; which plant is taller, what toy is heavier, how far can you throw the ball?

As a starting point, some examples of mathematical language and concepts often used during tasks and activities are given below:

- measurements – time, height, weight, large (larger, largest), small (smaller, smallest), volume, length, different measures and overall size

- length – long (longer, longest), short, (shorter, shortest), full length, same length

- width – narrow (narrower, narrowest), wide (wider, widest), thin (thinner, thinnest), thick (thicker, thickest), same width

- volume – amount, contain (contains, container), full (fuller, fullest), empty (emptier, emptiest), deep (deeper, deepest), shallow (shallower, shallowest), fits, hold

- distance – near (nearer, nearest), far (farther, farthest), close (closer, closest), alongside, side by side, between, beside

- overall size – full, all, final, together, combined

- patterns and sequences – different, same, first, last, next, repeat, match, again

- other words – guess, estimate, different, same, equal, amount, comparison, contrast, part of, most, least.

Numbers, Counting, Estimating and Keeping Score/Tally

Children can learn about numbers in many more ways other than just learning to count by rote. During play and physical activities children will often be counting, estimating and keeping score. Estimating will help children to eventually get closer to the accurate numbers. Keeping score will help children to make sense of the numbers, counting steps/throws/spins will make much more sense than just counting.

Patterns and Sequences

In a pattern, there are always elements that repeat in an obvious and predictable way, based on a mathematical rule. When something repeats, such as 1,2,3,4,5, 1,2,3,4,5, this will teach children about patterns and sequences. Children will learn patterns when playing clapping games, making repeated movements to music, taking part in active stories with a pattern that repeats and active rhymes. You can use the patterns in music and poetry beats, for example, soft, soft, loud, soft, soft, loud.

Counting may seem simple to adults, but it can be difficult for children if they are taught numbers as symbols, rather than giving numbers meaning. Using numbers and sequences of numbers in games, songs and rhymes will broaden children's knowledge of what number follows next.

Top Tip – Repeated movements through obstacle courses and follow-the-leader, e.g. jump forward, jump backward and hop, jump forward, jump backward and hop, are some ideas of activities with patterns and sequences.

Shapes and Space

Recognising shapes and how they fit together is another aspect of mathematical learning. Children need to recognise and form geometrical shapes and discover the shapes that are everywhere. Learning how to fit and manipulate shapes will increase their understanding of our world and how it is structured and designed. Puzzles, as well as building and construction, help us to understand how we can use and manipulate shapes. Being active also helps to develop better spatial awareness, which is vitally important for mathematics and problem-solving.

Top Tip – Activities where children make shapes with their bodies help with the understanding of shapes in the world and at the same time, help children develop an awareness of their own bodies and what they are capable of doing physically.

Sorting

Sorting objects into sizes, colours, shapes, and just about anything else will lead to children's later ability to divide, add, categorise and count. Sorting makes sense of groups of objects, people or animals and makes them more manageable to either count, divide or categorise. Children often naturally create their own sorting activities and we can enhance this with games such as four corners – can you put the same colour/shaped object in the corner with the same colour/shape as quickly as you can? Tidying up at the end of an activity session will usually also require children to do sorting.

Comparing and Contrasting

Using real-world personal objects and ourselves will help children to understand differences. Who is taller, how many girls, who has bigger shoes, how many have blonde hair? If you have 10 fingers, jump into a hoop; if you are four years old, hop on one foot. We can also use everyday objects to compare colour, size, shape, etc.

Environment and Risky Play

Risk taking and challenges support mathematics. How high did you climb? Was it higher or lower than the last time you did that climb? Children will learn so much just from being outdoors or in a stimulating indoor environment.

Problem-Solving

A problem is something that you do not know how to solve and if someone else solves it for you then you will not have learnt how to solve that problem. A problem for one child may not be a problem for another child; the solution to a problem for one child may differ from the solution for another child.

Children will naturally set and solve problems and, in an environment that challenges them and with adults who question and discuss problems, they will develop strong problem-solving strategies. The more experiences children have the greater their ability to problem solve will become.

Purposeful play underpins problem-solving as children will be faced with new challenges and will find the need to use mathematical thinking and understanding. Developing knowledge by making mistakes is part of the process of problem-solving. Children will explore the problem, try a solution, if the solution fails, they will reflect and try a new solution until they have solved the problem. This is the basis for learning in early years and the process will be more meaningful and effective if it is delivered through enjoyment and play.

Spatial Awareness

Through exploring the environment, body awareness activities, activities where they need to judge distance and size and many activities where children need to fit themselves or others into a space, children develop their spatial awareness. Without good spatial awareness children will struggle with many mathematical concepts, particularly those that include volume, area and space. They will find reproducing patterns, sequences and shapes difficult. Encouraging good spatial awareness will help a child with many day-to-day tasks and mathematical skills.

Children also need to understand concepts such as value, borrowing, division, time and problem-solving, which can be learnt and discovered through many activities, movement to music and exploration of the environment.

PHYSICAL ACTIVITY IDEAS

Generally, when children are moving and being active, they are learning mathematical concepts, not only when doing activities with a particular mathematical focus. Below are examples of some of the types of activities that support learning in this area:

- active stories that include numbers and mathematics
- active rhymes that include numbers and numbering
- action songs
- gardening and food growing
- cooking/food preparation – counting, measuring, recording, reason-ing and following instructions
- local area and the world – going for walks, map making
- building and construction – including simple towers, dens, bridges and other 3D structures
- treasure and scavenger hunts

- weighing, measuring and comparing size games, including using non-standard measures
- bubbles, water play
- mud play (mud kitchen)
- number activities
- scoring
- grouping and dividing
- simple experiments
- collecting and sorting
- activities with sequences or patterns
- comparing and contrasting activities
- use of positional and directional language.

Ideas

Activities from Chapter 11 that support this area of learning include the following activities:

- * Active Cube
- * Active Stories
- * Aim and Score
- * Ball Stop
- * Beanbag Relay Races
- * Cone Catches
- * Fantastic Elastic (see below)
- * Movement to Music and Dance Ideas
- * Musical Groups
- * Number Hunts
- * Number Circle
- * Paper Fortune Teller

Fantastic Elastic

Fantastic Elastic is a simple resource – a circle made from thick elastic, approximately four meters in length.

Through Fantastic Elastic activities, children will not only learn about numbers but also a variety of mathematical concepts such as shapes, problem-solving, positions and positional language, and comparing and contrasting. The elastic can be used to create many activities, enhance activities and help children to focus and concentrate.

Children can learn about shapes by working as a group to create a triangle, square or rectangle out of the elastic. Through positional activities they can develop a better understanding of over, under, around and above, etc.; they can also learn in groups about numbers, division, addition and grouping. Ideas of how to use Fantastic Elastic can be found in Chapter 11.

Top Tip – Start slowly with younger children, repeat the simple moves and add new ones from time to time.

Top Tip – Maximum 10–15 children in a Fantastic Elastic group. The older and more able the children are, the larger the group can be.

Mini Moves, Animals and Numbers

When children are young we love to teach them to count and find it exciting when they reach the milestones of counting to 10 or 20. These are great accomplishments, however even if a child can count to 10, it does not necessarily mean they understand the meaning of numbers, what they are used for and how they are sequenced.

Activities that place numbers in context are important to help children understand how they fit into the real world. Using imagination, music, energy and fun, children can learn about and come to understand numbers.

Anyone who works with young children will quickly realise that they love to engage in games with an animal theme and the 10 Mini Moves cards with an animal on one side and number on the other side are perfect for this (see Chapter 11). They can be used to create simple activities such as Number Hunts or Number Circles (see Chapter 11). Including questions and discussions can help children use their higher thinking skills and start to make sense of numbers. This can be done while seated – but they will learn so much more if they are moving and having fun!

Shared Practice

2D shapes

By Jenny Gibson

I have been teaching for 27 years, mostly in infant schools, and for the past 14 years I have taught Reception and Year 1 together. I attended one of Tania's courses a few years ago and was inspired!

Resources

Different shaped mats, for example, circle, square, triangle, rectangle.

Idea 1

For the warm-up children 'walk the shape', such as:

- walk in the shape of a rectangle (4 steps)
- walk in the shape of a triangle (1 step in front, 2 behind).

Hold the shapes up for the children to see as they are 'walking' them. Alternatively, a child can hold the shape up.

Idea 2

Draw shapes in chalk on the ground and children walk over them, stepping on each corner. Alternatively, draw large shapes and they can take many steps to walk it out.

Idea 3

They can play follow-the-leader as a class and make huge shapes.

Idea 4

They could stretch arm muscles by drawing big shapes in the air as they are held up and calling out the name of the shape.

Idea 5

Lay out all the shape mats and play energetic music. Children walk, run, skip, gallop around them. When the music stops or on a signal they jump onto a mat. Give instructions, for example, if you are on a triangle put your hand in the air, if you are on a circle sit down, etc.

Idea 6

Put one shape in each corner of the room. Say run to the...build up suspense...triangle corner (or hop to the square corner, slide to the rectangle corner, etc). This can get a bit hectic but is usually fun and children can learn about avoiding one another if it is talked about first or introduced with instructions to run, but without touching anyone.

Children can cool down with 'guess the shape' in which an adult or child either draws a large shape in the air or 'walks' the shape. The others have to guess which shape it is and copy it.

The children could continue this activity in their play if offered chalks and shape mats on another day.

Benefits

These activities support gross motor development, spatial aware-ness, mathematics, language, communication and thinking skills.

Chapter 4

LANGUAGE, LITERACY AND COMMUNICATION

Physical activities are a powerful way to develop children's communication skills, language and literacy. It is much easier for them to understand what words mean if they are used in context of an active story or role play and using flash cards during activities can help them get their heads around what the words mean. Furthermore, discussions during activities that are challenging or involve problem-solving can develop communication skills.

Active Stories

Language Role Modelling

Worded Flashcards

Turn Taking
for conversation

**Role-play, Imagination
and Verbalisation**

**Alphabet and
Letter Activities**

Cooperative Play

Phonic Activities

Active Rhymes
using repetition and
new words

Spatial Awareness
for writing

Action Learning

**Gross & Fine
Motor Development**

Active Story Composition

Large Painting

Drawing to Music

Brain Development

Top Tip – The language that is used at home and in nurseries is quite informal and very different to the more formal language used in school and some preschools. It is important to be aware of the differences in these two styles of language and of the way these differences can impact on children's ability to understand and communicate when starting school. Use fun activities with more formal language and instructions to bridge the gap.

HOW PHYSICAL ACTIVITY IMPACTS CHILDREN'S LANGUAGE, LITERACY AND COMMUNICATION

Physical activities in groups and pairs develop children's communication and language, and incorporating stories and imagination extends children's understanding and use of language.

- Communication develops through teamwork, discussions and cooperative play.

- Adults can be used as role models – children follow simple gestures and body language used by adults during all kinds of group activities and social interactions.

- Developing words and language through physical activities can be a useful tool for teaching children who are learning a second language and children who are developing their language skills alike.

- Active rhymes allow children to learn new language through repetition and learn the rhythm of language.

- Children can listen, recall, ask questions and carry out instructions when playing and being physically active.

- Communication happens through enjoyment – children are more likely to communicate if they are happy and relaxed.

- Children can learn about taking turns during conversation – turn taking is a skill learnt while playing and being active in pairs and groups.

- Simple concepts such as big/small can be learnt through actions. Positional language is learnt in order for children to follow instructions.

- Active stories can be used to explain, use tenses and develop vocabulary and use of narrative. They can also develop their writing skills through opportunity to create their own written story.

- Play can be used to explain simple gestures. Research has shown that children learn language faster if they can see gestures made by adults when they are talking.

- Children can learn to follow direction (Simon Says, obstacle course, active stories, games, etc.).

- Role play will involve using vocabulary to verbalise imaginative play.

- Play can help children understand the difference between factual and imaginative play.

- The meaning and sounds of words can be explained through actions.

- Play can incorporate language and culturally important activities (e.g. folk talks and songs).

- Through discussions, children will be able to understand how to verbalise what they are doing.

- Children will learn by communicating their activity ideas with adults and other children.

- Development of language skills will occur through being involved in the storyline of active stories.

- Children can react to activities provided via various media, e.g. musical CDs, activity films on the internet.

- Active stories and other activities can helps children to sequence sentences into short narratives.

- Encouraging children to verbally ponder on challenges will lead to more use of and development of language skills.

Reading

- Encourage reading and language skills through imaginative play.

- Use written stories to prompt active stories.

- Act out rhymes, songs, poems and jingles.
- Contribute to stories (e.g. change endings).
- Use word cards to prompt actions, such as skills, animals, fruit, etc.
- Act out words to help children understand their meaning.
- Use alphabet games and phonic games to develop reading skills.

Writing

- Use alphabet games and phonic games to develop writing skills.
- Use placement of written work on a page to develop spatial awareness.
- Children can create their own active stories, writing them down or writing key words such as the main character, the animals, the names, etc.
- Gross motor skill activities, such as large painting, will help develop fine motor skills.
- Paint and draw to music.

Children require a lot more than just fine motor skills to write. Other important components for effective writing are posture and balance for hand and arm control; strong muscles in their back, stomach, neck and shoulders to support refined hands and finger skills; bilateral coordination (the use of both hands at the same time); spatial awareness to organise what is on the page, and hand-eye coordination to guide their hand across the page. These are all developed through play in early years, hence forcing children to sit down and write too soon will hinder rather than help their ability to write.

When children play with others they develop their verbal skills, communication skills and language, and also an understanding of how to communicate and the language that they are using. Through cooperation and communication when playing, children learn how to sequence, structure and order words to make a sentence that others will understand and react to. Young children will follow our lead when communicating, they will try out the rules of conversation that we use. They will break the rules and eventually discover how to communicate effectively by using the accepted rules of that particular language. Through music and rhymes, preferably active versions to make them more enjoyable, children will learn about the rhythm of language and word structure. Rhymes also teach children more words, especially through repetition and this repetition will also give them the opportunity to master these words.

In the English language there are 44 sounds (phonemes) which are combined to form words. These sounds are made up of:

- 25 consonant sounds

- 19 vowel sounds

  - 5 long vowels

  - 5 short vowels

  - 3 diphthongs

  - 2 'oo' sounds

  - 4 'r' controlled vowels.

The number of phonemes in the other major European languages are: German has 46, French has 34, Spanish has 24, Italian has 49 and Portuguese has 38.

Many children initially learn language through phonics, starting with the sounds which will eventually be combined into words and, in turn, sentences. There are many fun active ways, games and activities to teach phonics, enhancing children's enjoyment of learning language.

Supporting the development of language and communication with active rhymes, active stories, role play, movement to music and action songs will lay a strong foundation for children to tackle writing and expressing their thoughts and ideas through written word.

NATURAL DEVELOPMENT

Examples of how children will learn language and communication through self-directed movement and active play in the early years include:

- building a den, which involves communicating with each other as to what is needed, how they would like it to look and who is doing each task

- pretending to be a dragon, a pirate or a fish, role playing also involves communicating with each other about who they are and what they are doing

- answering and asking questions as they try to construct a structure, on their own or with other children

- reflecting or verbally processing out loud

- discovering names and classifications of plants, places, animals and minibeasts as they explore new places

- developing their fine motor skills and the gross motor skills that support all kinds of active play, such as climbing, digging, picking up small natural objects and making marks in mud, sand and gravel

- being engaged in large painting outside, on paper or with water on just about anything

- tidying up before lunch or the end of the day, discussing what should be placed where.

FINE MOTOR DEVELOPMENT

Children require building blocks to lay the foundation before acquiring fine motor control. These building blocks include:

- stability – strength and balance allowing one part of the body to stay still while the other moves

- sensation – awareness of the placement of your fingers, hands and arms and how they are moving

- bilateral coordination – both hands being involved in separate aspects of a task.

The building blocks – stability, sensation and bilateral coordination – are developed from birth through movement and play. Tummy time, crawling, running, moving to music, exploring different objects, textures and materials, and many more movements contribute to this.

Children also need to be able to plan, have an awareness of what they are doing and develop a properly mature nervous system, along with coordination and strong muscles in their back, stomach, neck and shoulders to support refined hand and finger skills.

Once the building blocks have been established, children develop dexterity. They will be able to use small, accurate, and precise movements to complete various day-to-day tasks.

You will find more information about bilateral coordination in Chapter 1.

MUSCLE STRENGTH

It is important to develop shoulder muscle strength, which provides stability for the smaller muscles in the hands and arms. This will prevent children from getting tired when writing and cutting with scissors, so get those babies on their stomachs and get children active.

Children should have access to large equipment which not only develops the gross motor skills that underpin fine motor skills, but also develops skills such as gripping, turning and manipulating.

Top Tip – Give children ribbons, scarves or fabric when moving to music. This will encourage them to move their arms from their shoulders, developing their shoulder muscles (see Ribbon Dance in Chapter 11).

RELUCTANT CHILDREN

Many young children, particularly boys, would rather be playing outside with a ball than sitting still drawing or threading beads. It is therefore wise to let children burn off energy before sitting down to do fine motor activities or slip fine motor activities into or in-between gross motor activities.

Use active stories that will get children moving. You might consider getting the children to pretend to be a character or animal that will do large energetic moves as well as fine motor tasks – a monkey swinging through the trees then eating a banana, or squirrel scampering over the ground to his supply of acorns.

Top Tip – Include a fine motor task in an obstacle course, such as a section where they will need to thread a number of beads, pick up the same colour of pompoms with tongs and place in another container, etc.

FINE MOTOR FOUNDATION SKILLS

In preparation for school, children will need a solid foundation of fine motor skills in order for them to be able to write and use scissors.

Foundation skills to prepare children for writing

- Posture and balance for hand and arm control
- Grasping strength and finger control for appropriate grip on a writing implement
- Ocular motor control in order for hand and eyes to move together
- Being able to following instructions
- Being able to pay attention
- The ability to recall correctly
- Spatial organisation

Foundation skills to prepare children for cutting with scissors

- Postural control
- The ability to open and close the hand
- Bilateral coordination where the one hand is the 'doing' hand and the other is the 'helping' hand
- Being able to isolate fingers to move independently from each other
- Hand-eye coordination
- Stability

MUSIC AND BIG RHYMES

Music helps children to understand the rhythm of language. Through movement to music, children can develop rhythm and understanding of how words fit together and work in sentences. When music is linked with language it is a powerful tool to support the learning of language.

Big rhymes, where we act out rhymes energetically, are a great way to introduce new words and the rhythm of language to children. Usually rhymes are repetitive, benefitting the need for children to repeat what they do and hear to learn and retain the information. Once children have developed a bank of words they will need to hear an array of words, rather than repeating the same ones, in order to develop their vocabulary. It is important to be aware of what words children already know, reinforcing the correct use of these and then adding to them.

IMAGINATIVE PLAY AND ROLE PLAY

Using imagination to encourage more movement and active play can also support the development of language skills in young children. Children's language will grow from listening to stories, and their linguistic skills will be greatly enhanced when given the opportunity to contribute to a story or to create their own story. Active stories give children the opportunity to explore their own thoughts and feelings and a medium to express them.

Role play will introduce new words, communication and use of language in a context that makes sense.

ROLE MODELLING AND COMMUNICATING

Children learn through role modelling, and our use of language and communication during imaginative play and regular physical activities will help children to develop their own abilities. They need to understand instructions in order to follow them so it is important for adults to be aware of how children communicate.

When having conversations with children, introduce new words and variation of words commonly used. Also make use of more challenging language as well as complex sentences to widen children's exposure to language. This can be adapted to children's ability, making your sentence structure less or more complex; however, it is important to challenge them.

Top Tip – When planning skills of the week, use flashcards and as many variations of a word as possible, such as jump, jumping, jumped, jumps. This will help children learn new words and put them into context through performing the skill; by using them in active stories and rhymes, they will learn about sequencing of sentences.

CONVERSATION RATHER THAN QUESTIONS

Rather than constantly asking children questions, it is more beneficial to engage in conversation with them. This could be general conversation, discussions about what they are doing, how they are going to achieve their expected outcome, what they want to do next, etc. When interactions are more conversational, children will have more opportunity to broaden their language skills, with support from adults, who should use these occasions to use more complex sentence sequences and new words.

OUTDOOR PLAY

It has become common knowledge that outdoor play is important for children's physical development and learning. Children's language can develop naturally as they run, make a noise and explore outside. Using language alongside movement and active play (inside and out) will give children many opportunities to try new words and sounds in a fun and enjoyable way.

PHYSICAL ACTIVITY IDEAS

Here is an outline of some of the types of activities that support learning in this area:

- active stories – context of words, follow what adult says, children have the opportunity to create the story or contribute to the story, children communicate with each other
- active rhymes – teach children about language and the rhythm of language
- flashcards – can read words on flashcards and act out the words, e.g. cards with words or images of animals, fruit, weather, plants, vehicles.

- movement to music – learn rhythms which prepare children for the rhythm of language, instruction-based moves/dance, moving in pairs, groups
- story dances – movement that follows elements of a story
- activities in pairs or groups that require communication with each other
- imaginative play – activities that include imagination, animals, superheroes, etc.
- following instructions from adults and copying their language
- learn about taking turns, which teaches children about taking turns when communicating
- role play – good for language and communication
- treasure and scavenger hunts
- alphabet and phonic games
- large painting, drawing and mark making
- painting or drawing to music.

Ideas

Activities from Chapter 11 that support this area of learning include the following activities:

- * Active Alphabets
- * Active Cube
- * Active Stories
- * Ball Stop
- * Bigger! 'Head shoulders knees and toes'
- * Cats and Rabbits
- * Cone Catches
- * Colours
- * Fantastic Elastic
- * Letter Run Around
- * Magic Rocks and the Giant (Hide the Spot!)
- * Mini Yo! (or other yoga-based resources)
- * Monkey Madness

* Movement to Music and Dances Ideas
  * Musical Statue Champions
  * In pairs
  * Feather Dance
  * Listen and Move
  * Ribbon Dance
  * Dancing Stories
* Musical Groups
* Number Circle
* Paper Fortune Teller
* Props
* Shadows
* Slow Mo
* Superheroes to the Rescue
* The Boat (Mini Yo! or other yoga-based cards)

Mini Yo!

Working with children in early years, I discovered that active stories through yoga moves were very popular amongst the young children and a great way to encourage more movement and interaction.

Initially I used various yoga resources available to purchase but, even though they were great, I was constantly adapting them to make them suitable for younger children. I came to realise that I had been developing a new yoga resource through my various interactions with children in early years. And so, Mini Yo! was born.

Mini Yo! is a simple pack of colourful cards, each with a different simplified yoga move. Each card has an image of the move, as well as its name, allowing children to identify what you say with the written word. An explanation of the move and its benefits are found on the back of each card, allowing anyone to pick up the pack and use it.

Yoga is commonly thought to be a calm, relaxing activity, which is how Mini Yo! can be used. However, using a selection of moves (three or four) together to create a story can encourage gross motor movement, use of imagination, language and communication, creativity and a love of being active. Young children enjoy being aeroplanes, standing on one foot with their wings spread out to the side. This can be a challenging pose for many young children; however, it is surprising how quickly they will develop if given enough opportunity to practice. They love to pretend to be trees, standing very still on one foot or one foot and toes of the other foot, waving their branches about in the wind, falling when being chopped down and growing back up. It is important for children to move from slow to fast to still, up and down, backwards and forwards to support the development of body control. Children love meowing like cats or roaring like lions, which is very energising, and they also enjoy curling up, pretending to be a rock at the end of a session, calming them down in preparation for their next class or activity.

Unexpectedly, Mini Yo!, which was developed with early years children in mind, is being used by many teachers with older children. Teachers have been using the resource to provide children the opportunity to create and write their own Mini Yo! stories and to enjoy the ownership of their own activity.

Mini Yo! has proven not only to support the development of young children's balance and strength but is also stimulating their minds, creativity, understanding of the world, social interaction and helping them to enjoy being active. Please see more about the benefits of yoga-based activities in the Shared Practice section in Chapter 2.[1]

MINI YO! IN AFRICA

I spent a morning at Orban School, a bilingual community school in Johannesburg, South Africa, delivering Mini Yo! activities. As it was a hot, sunny day, 40 children from the school joined me in stretching, balancing and trying out various Mini Yo! poses outside. They were then split into small groups, given three different Mini Yo! cards each and challenged to create a story, which they performed for the full group at the end of the session.

The school staff encourage outdoor activities and play on a daily basis, however they benefited from learning about language development through physical activities. The children enjoyed being creative with their stories and loved the physical aspect of it. Oh, and you could definitely tell who were the competitive children in the school.

I thoroughly enjoyed experiencing Mini Yo! Africa style and loved seeing how much the children enjoyed being imaginative and creative.

---

1 You can find out more about this resource at www.binspireduk.co.uk/resources.

Shared Practice

Active Stories and Themed Circuits

By Jenny Griffin

I have been a teacher for four years and have taught both Early Years Foundation Stage and Key Stage 1. I love teaching physical education and now use a lot of active stories to accompany my lessons and incorporate Mini Yo! positions, following the training I attended delivered by Tania. This week we learnt the 'p' sound in phonics and we have Pirate Pete story books in class, so the theme of the warm-up was Pirate Pete who makes a 'p' sound. We used Mini Yo! moves to be the boat (the rusty bucket), a treasure chest, a one legged pirate who had a sword fight with a 'warrior' who had a 'cat'! The children loved it and there were lots of opportunities to incorporate floor and standing balances. We will keep this going for a few weeks as children develop and add to the story.

Now that I am used to using the yoga moves I am finding it much easier to be creative about what each yoga position can become. Below are some other ideas I have used.

Idea 1 – Dinosaur and Mini Beast Circuits

I've linked fundamental movements to both dinosaurs and mini beasts using fast based circuit activities, such as asking the children to come up with an animal and then thinking about how it might move, then with a little adult input link it to some of the movements I want the children to work on.

We spent a minute on each activity with 30 seconds break and then gradually increased the time/challenge.

Idea 2 – Bear Hunt PE

The other activity they've loved is having a literacy-themed lesson, so when we did *We're Going on a Bear Hunt* we had 'bear' physical education. All the children brought in a bear and we used the story plus some bear-themed rhymes and songs and the parachute to link it all together, such as: 'Ten little teddy bears jumping on the bed' (bears on the parachute) and 'round and round the garden like a teddy bear' (children moved with their bears in different ways).

Idea 3 - Assault Courses

Finally as part of our healthy living topic children had a gym role play and then outdoors I provided lots of tyres, planks, stepping stones, etc. and the children loved building their own assault course (this really developed balancing skills and was completely child-initiated). The children added their own challenge of completing the circuit without touching the ground.

Benefits

These activities support gross motor development, language, communication, expressive arts and design, creative development, knowledge of, and understanding the world, PSED, mathematics, problem-solving and thinking skills.

Chapter 5

PERSONAL, SOCIAL AND EMOTIONAL DEVELOPMENT (PSED)

Playing with other children and adults is a child's first social experience. They learn how to interact with each other with respect, how to communicate and cooperate, share and take turns. They develop creativity, independence, and an awareness of how to cope with winning and losing, important life lessons that prepare them for future participation in sports, day-to-day tasks and interactions, as well as general challenges they may face in their lives.

Social Skills
through playing in groups and pairs

Feelings & Emotions
through active stories

Resilience
through focussing on the process, not just the outcome

Confidence
by overcoming challenges and achivements

Concentration
through regular activity

How to cope
with challenge and change through access to a variety of activities with challenges

Sense of Self & Body Awareness
through spatial awareness activities

Empathy & Compassion
through group activities

Stress Relief
through being active

Respect for Others
through group activities

Behavioural Impact
through regular physical activity

Free Expression
through self-directed play

HOW PHYSICAL ACTIVITY IMPACTS CHILDREN'S PERSONAL SOCIAL AND EMOTIONAL DEVELOPMENT

When children are playing and being active they are learning essential social skills and developing a sense of self and self-esteem through small achievements.

- When children reach new milestones or achieve what they set out to do it positively impacts their confidence and self-esteem. Many of these challenges occur when playing and being physically active.

- Children learning to persevere with a task or activity and discovering that failure is part of achievement helps them to build resilience.

- Young children learn important social skills through playing and taking part in physical activities in pairs and groups.

- Regular physical activity throughout the day helps concentration.

- Research has shown that being active supports stress relief and promotes relaxation. It can reduce fear, anxiety and irritability.

- Children are programmed to be active on a regular basis, therefore allowing them to move more will positively impact their behaviour.

- Play and physical activities are important tools to teach children the importance of their own health and well-being.

- Activities using our body parts, the space around us and others can help children to develop an understanding of their own bodies, self-awareness and self-worth.

- Interaction with others will support the ability to share with others, understand others, support others and develop empathy and compassion. It also helps children to become aware of the needs of others.

- Movement and active play in a group environment teaches children to understand emotions, respect and boundaries through enjoyable experiences.

- Encouraging children to understand and recognise their own achievements when playing supports self-esteem and resilience.

- Physical activity and play help children learn to positively respond to challenges and manage change.

- Group activities help children to respond well to responsibility.

- Through physical activities young children learn about inclusion and the differences and similarities of groups, such as culture, religion, gender, disability, etc.

- Movement and active play help children to freely express their interests, opinions and needs.

- Children learn about turn taking, being patient and how not all outcomes will be as expected when being physically active, which are important life-long skills.

- Children learn about the importance of rules, right from wrong and consequences when playing and being active in groups.

- Movement and active play can heal emotional pain in a non-threatening manner.

- Children can learn about emotions and feelings through active stories and role play.

Studies have shown that physical activity and play stimulate the higher emotional regulating part of the brain,[1,2] leading to improved management of emotions and stress; they also increase attention span and help children to deal with frustration, which all have a positive impact on children's attainment at school. It was found that not only formal physical education lessons impact this but, more importantly, so do regular unstructured physical activity breaks, especially in the outdoors.

---

1 Play England (2008) 'Chapter 3: The Importance of Play in Children's Lives.' *Play for a Change*. Available at www.playengland.org.uk/resource/play-for-a-change-play-policy-and-practice-a-review-of-contemporary-perspectives accessed on 19 December 2016.

2 Pellegrini, A.D. and Bohn-Gettler, C.M. (2013) 'The benefits of recess in primary school.' *Scholarpedia 8*, 2, 30448.

Top Tip – Create a short energetic activity related to the area of learning to break up a lesson if children need to sit and focus. This will help them concentrate for longer and could enhance their learning.

CONFIDENCE AND SELF-ESTEEM

Ultimately, a child is the only person who can determine their self-esteem and confidence; however, it is up to the adults who care for them to provide an environment and level of activity to help them develop this. Providing activities that challenge but are not too difficult is important. A child who is not challenged can become bored and potentially develop bad behaviour, whereas a child who is unable to achieve what they are asked to do might give up or become frustrated, which could also lead to bad behaviour. Both these situations would have a negative impact on the child's self-esteem. Placed in the right environment, children have a huge capacity to develop their own self-esteem, confidence, resilience and problem-solving skills.

Top Tip – Differentiation during structured physical activities is very important at this age as children are developing at such different rates. Use tools such as PATTER (see Chapter 1) to help you to plan for different abilities. See Chapter 1 for more details.

The following ideas are some ways adults can support the development of children's confidence and self-esteem.

- Focus on the process rather than the outcome – children will learn more, allowing more opportunity for acknowledgement of achievements.

- Remember that young children are still developing in many ways, socially, emotionally and physically. Understanding their individual needs and abilities will help you to understand how to support them better.

- Create a positive attitude towards making mistakes and encourage perseverance.

- Let children complete their own tasks and only help if they ask for your help, if there is a threat of injury to them or others or if you feel a little help will teach them something useful and positive or move them on if stuck.

- Allow children to identify their own achievements, encourage them to reflect on what they have learnt and achieved and how they feel about the experience. This will have a greater impact on them than always telling them how well you feel they have done.

- Provide many open-ended opportunities, which will allow children's confidence to develop through leading activities and creating their own ideas.

- Make time for one-to-one activities and individual attention as positive relationships and attachments will underpin children's confidence as they venture out, explore and push themselves, ultimately leading to good self-esteem.

- Your behaviour and self-image will have an impact on the children in your care. Be a happy, involved, caring, confident role model.

Even as an adult, feeling a sense of achievement when completing a small or large task does wonders for our self-image and confidence. When a child catches a ball, when they complete an obstacle course, when they climb to the first or last branch of a tree, when they build a bridge from boxes, they learn what their capabilities are. When doing so with other children they will also learn to take turns, to communicate with others and interpret their emotions, to have respect for each other and how to lead and follow.

Setting small challenges on a regular basis will help children grow and develop. However, rather than always setting challenges yourself and rewarding when the challenges have been achieved, also support children to develop the ability to challenge themselves and identify their own achievements.

RESILIENCE

Resilience helps us cope with the challenges, difficulties and changes that life throws at us. It helps us be strong and face life with a positive attitude, even in difficult circumstances. Children who are resilient will be happier, be less likely to develop problems such as depression and anxiety and will be more likely to continue to deal with life positively into adulthood.

We need to support children to become more resilient through movement and active play.

- Let children learn that it is ok to make mistakes. Not always achieving at first and having to reflect and then problem-solve will help children to become stronger and cope with adversity throughout their lives.

- Provide small challenges building on previous achievements and remind them what they have done so far. This will help children move forward and use techniques that they have previously used to problem-solve and persevere.

- Allowing children to find physical activities that they really enjoy will not only underpin lifelong love of being physically active but will also help children learn about their abilities and challenge themselves more.

- Young children interact with other children when they play and are physically active. Through these interactions they develop positive relationships which play an important role in lifelong resilience.

- In the correct environment and with positive support, children can focus on what they can do rather than on what they cannot do. Resilient people do not spend too much time focusing on their 'failures', they pick themselves up and move forward.

- Interacting with children on activities that they enjoy will help you get to know them better and will be great for your relationship with them. Positive relationships with adults and other children underpin the development of resilience.

- Self-directed play, as well as giving children the opportunity to choose activities or play a part in creating activities, will give them a sense of responsibility, help them build decision-making skills and, in turn, lead to a more confident child.

- Planned physical activity sessions and physical education lessons will ensure that all children are included and will also help them try new activities, helping them to discover what they like and more about their own abilities. Be sure to differentiate when working with a group of children, allowing them to find their level of difficulty whilst still being challenged.

- Being physically active, along with eating well and having enough sleep, will help children to cope with daily challenges.

Children will miss all the small achievements throughout the process if they are focusing on the outcome and can become disheartened if the outcome is not as expected. Providing a safe and caring environment for children to problem-solve and make mistakes will help them push themselves and develop the confidence to try new things. Children learn so much from their mistakes and if they develop the ability to persevere, it will positively impact their resilience for the rest of their lives.

Do not underestimate children's abilities. If we believe in them they will believe in themselves and will also want to do better and be more inclined to want to please us. All children are different; we just need to give them to opportunity to find what they are good at and what they enjoy. In the right situation, all children will flourish.

BEHAVIOUR AND MENTAL HEALTH

We spend so much time asking children to sit still, be still and stop fidgeting, we sometimes forget that young children need to move to grow, develop and learn. Asking them to behave unnaturally could lead to negative behaviour. How many times while watching a young child playing, constantly on the go, do you think 'I wish I had that much energy'? They do have boundless energy and if we do not allow them to move, that energy will be channelled elsewhere, often turning into bad behaviour.

Remember that all children are different and have different life experiences leading up to the point where you first meet them. An only child may have had few opportunities at home to learn how to interact with others, to take turns and that they cannot always get what they want. These are skills that they need to learn so may need longer to get to grips with these concepts. In the same way an only child will be the first to be faced with new skills and experiences, a child who is the youngest sibling in a larger family may have had everything done for them and need to learn independence and decision-making, amongst many other skills. Once again, if you understand the child and what they have experienced in their lives so far, you will be better prepared to support their growth and development.

Children in early years have to learn about emotions and become emotionally literate. As all children are different, with different characters and life situations and experience, some may find it easy to 'fit in', whereas others might take a long time to develop emotional literacy. These children may 'explode' or appear to behave badly on a regular basis.

Top Tip – Provide activities that help children to understand their feelings, such as role play, active stories and games that include emotions such as happy, sad and angry. Children will find this fun and non-threatening.

Creative play and physical activity also play a role in the development of executive function skills and self-regulation, which are needed to control emotions and cope with difficult situations. Through movement and active play, especially outside, children can express anger, be destructive and generally express emotions that are not usually acceptable in most situations. Giving children the freedom to express themselves and their emotions will also help them to learn about acceptable behaviour.

Tips for Behaviour Management

- Praise children. Of course, as adults who care for children, you will find yourself happily praising them on a regular basis. But there will be times when children may be attention seeking through negative behaviour. Attention seeking is a sign that there is an issue, such as low self-esteem, issues at home or lack of positive relationships. Distracting children from this behaviour by praising something else they have done or are doing can diffuse the situation, while reinforcing your relationship.

- Encourage children to identify their achievements and to praise themselves.

- Use positive language. Be mindful to avoid negative language or harsh use of your voice. Children learn so much more from us than what we teach them.

- Make physical activities, or any other form of activity, engaging and appropriate.

- Differentiate to allow for all children's abilities, enjoyment and engagement.

- Partake in activities and have fun with the children to develop a positive relationship and model good behaviour.

- Avoid preferential treatment of individual children but, where possible, allow for one-to-one time.

- Have realistic expectations of children. The more you understand their needs, abilities and interests the better.

- Create opportunities for self-regulation through regular risky play.

EMOTIONAL LITERACY

Young children need to be taught about their feelings to help them make sense of their emotions. This will allow them to become adults who can express themselves appropriately, regulate how they behave in social situations, and who are compassionate and empathetic.

Top Tip – Active stories, songs and active rhymes about feelings are great activities to help children understand their emotions. They will also learn through generally being active and playing in groups.

SELF-REGULATION

Self-regulation is defined as the ability to identify and control our own behaviour, emotions, and thinking; and the ability to amend these to allow us to respond appropriately to various situations. Challenging situations are opportunities to teach children perseverance, patience and understanding of themselves. Self-regulation usually refers to emotions and behaviour; however, self-regulation can be learnt through, and is useful for, physical activities as children need to discover what their limits are and how far they can push and challenge themselves.

There is a growing body of research showing that children playing outside regularly are more able to self-regulate.[3, 4] Outdoor play also helps children to be calmer, develop their language skills and have fewer behaviour issues.

INDEPENDENCE

Ultimately, we want children to become independent adults. In order to develop independence, children need to learn self-belief. Supporting children to feel good about themselves and their abilities, giving them responsibilities and allowing them to learn from their mistakes without making a fuss will lead to independent young children and, in turn, adults.

Self-directed play is important for children to develop their self-belief. It is also important to give them responsibility and the opportunity to contribute to activities. Do we need a large body of research (of which there is plenty) to understand this or is it not apparent when experiencing time with children outside?

NATURAL DEVELOPMENT

Examples of how children will learn PSED through self-directed movement and active play in the early years include the following:

- When children are climbing they will be concentrating, problem-solving, learning to believe in themselves and their own ability. They will challenge themselves. When they reach the top or the desired place, they will feel a sense of achievement which will help their confidence grow. Children might become fearful, but if they push forward, with or without encouragement from

3   Play England (2008) 'Chapter 3: The Importance of Play in Children's Lives.' *Play for a Change*. Available at www.playengland.org.uk/resource/play-for-a-change-play-policy-and-practice-a-review-of-contemporary-perspectives, accessed on 19 December 2016.

4   Pellegrini, A.D. and Bohn-Gettler, C.M. (2013) 'The benefits of recess in primary school.' *Scholarpedia 8*, 2, 30448.

others, they will develop resilience and discover that they can do more than they thought.

- They will be learning about others and the social world through role play, imaginative play and active stories.

- They will be exploring nature, which can help them feel calm and free to express themselves physically and emotionally.

- They will be throwing and kicking balls and when the ball lands where they intended, or they manage to catch it, they will feel a sense of achievement.

- When throwing balls or an object to others and catching it when thrown back they will need to communicate with the other child, respect their space by not throwing the ball in their face or too hard and abide by the agreed social rules for the activity.

- They will be attempting obstacles courses and trim trails, which will give them a great sense of achievement and self-worth.

- They will play games with others cooperatively, learning to share, take turns and respect each other. Through playing with other children and playing enjoyable games in groups or pairs, children are learning social skills.

- The outdoor environment offers many open-ended opportunities to explore their own ability, create and try something new.

- When building with construction toys and/or natural resources children will need to problem solve, make various decisions and find making mistakes acceptable and part of the experience.

- They will be running, jumping, climbing, crawling, leaping, hopping, which will develop their agility, balance, coordination and spatial awareness (ABCS). Children will become more proficient at physical activities as well as many day-to-day tasks, supporting the development of confidence and self-esteem, being involved in social situations, becoming independent and resilient. Children need many opportunities to be active in order to develop appropriately and to allow them to interact as equals with their peers. If they are behind their peers developmentally this can have a negative impact on their self-esteem, which they can carry with them for the rest of their lives.

- They will be using real-world tools which will build their confidence as they are trusted to use the same implements as the adults in their lives. This will also teach them self-discipline, as they should be taught that these tools can be dangerous. They will also develop independence as they are being trusted and given responsibility.

SOCIAL SKILLS

Movement and active play include many occasions where children will be in pairs and groups, both during self-directed and adult-led activities. They will discover the rules of engaging with others through solving various social questions, such as Who will lead? Who will follow? Will we work together? Who can be involved? What shall we do?

Children will learn to cooperate with each other and other adults, and contribute to a group outcome not just their own needs. They will learn about compromise, self-regulation, self-awareness, compassion, empathy and respect and will develop the emotional intelligence and sense of belonging that they will require throughout their lives.

They also need to understand and respect other's space and boundaries, which is learnt through social interaction when we are young. They need to develop good spatial awareness which will allow them to be aware of where they are in relation to others. If children do not have enough exposure to movement and play in the early years or have a medical condition that affects their perspective, they may not develop good spatial awareness.

Young children need to learn how to interact with others in a group environment and also need to learn to understand their own and others' emotions. Many of these skills are learnt through movement and play in groups and pairs. They will also learn a lot of these skills through interaction with adults and by following their lead. Here is a list of the social and emotional skills young children need to learn and develop:

Being seen

Caring

Challenging

Copying

Creativity

Decision-making

Describing/talking about activities

Discussing

Dressing and undressing

Empathy

Encouraging

Engaging

Engaging in pairs/ groups/teams

Enjoyment

Evaluating

Exploring

Feeding back

Following

Following rules

Greeting

Holding

Independence

Interacting

Leading

Listening

Meeting and parting

Mimicking

Mirroring

Moving at different times

Moving at the same time

Praising

Problem-solving

Problem-solving with others

Reflecting

Remembering

Repeating

Respecting

Responsibility

Score keeping

Seeing

Self-awareness

Self-care

Sharing

Spontaneity

Trusting

Turn-taking

Watching

PHYSICAL ACTIVITY IDEAS

Physical activities that support personal, social and emotional development are endless. Following is an outline of some of the types of activities that support learning in this area:

- action songs
- active rhymes
- active stories
- activities where children can contribute
- activities where children feel a sense of achievement
- body awareness activities

- emotional literacy activities
- group activities
- my senses activities

Ideas

Activities from Chapter 11 that support this area of learning include the following activities:

* Active Alphabets
* Active Cube
* Active Stories
* Aim and Score
* Ball Stop
* Beanbag Relay Races
* Big Nursery Rhymes
* Cone Catches
* Fantastic Elastic
* Mini Yo! (or other yoga-based resources)
* Monkey Madness
* Movement to Music and Dances Ideas
  - Musical Statue Champions
  - In pairs
  - Feather Dance
  - Listen and Move
  - Ribbon Dance
  - Dancing Stories
* Musical Groups
* Number Circle
* Paper Fortune Teller
* Props
* Shadows
* Superheroes to the Rescue

Kevin the Superhero

I spent a day at an inner-city school in Birmingham, delivering activity sessions with their two reception classes and two Key Stage 1 classes in their outdoor area. I delivered high impact activities with the children, full of imagination, physical skills and yoga-based stories.

The second reception class joined me in the outdoor area, with an additional teacher. A teacher who was joining in to support Kevin, who had Down's Syndrome. Kevin enjoyed the physical activities with his classmates, trying out new moves and discovering new ways to use his body. He loved all the activities, however, when engaging in the Superheroes to the Rescue activity, he almost could not contain himself.

The Superheroes to the Rescue activity is a very energetic activity, where we pretend to be superheroes that fly to different parts of the world, running around the whole outdoor area, saving people and other living things (please see the full activity in Chapter 11). Each of us decided what hero we wanted to be, stood in our superhero pose on our spots to recharge our superpowers and raised our arms in the air, like Superman, to fly around. Kevin so loved being a superhero, when all the children walked back to their classroom at the end of the session, he insisted on flying like a superhero.

Active stories create exciting engaging activities for children. They are inclusive, allowing children to engage at a level that is suitable for them and different children can take on different responsibilities, such as being involved in the storyline or supporting other children who are not as physically developed as them.

Kevin was seen as someone who was moderately active and often would not fully engage. His physical ability was generally considered to be behind that of his peers and therefore he required additional support. As Kevin loved to pretend he was a superhero and as all children were able to engage at their own level, during the Superheroes to the Rescue activity he was able to engage independently and feel completely included. Irrespective of whether a child has a medical condition or just has not had enough opportunity to develop physically, it is important to provide many activities that will include children of varying abilities. Feeling part of the group is very important for a child's sense of self-worth and they will learn from each other, communicate with each other and support each other while having fun together.

Shared Practice

Body Awareness and Imaginative Movement

Lewis Miller

I have been a Sports Coach for nine years, and have worked in Europe and America. I now run Cool Skillz, providing sport and physical activity programmes and services for a variety of educational settings. I attended one of Tania's training courses a few years ago and have used much of what I learned from her in my practice as well as shared my practice with her.

Idea 1 – Body Ball
Give children a small ball each and get them to familiarise themselves with it.

- Roll the ball on different body parts.

- Roll the ball around one leg and then the other.

- Roll the ball around the stomach.

- Roll the ball on the floor in a figure of eight.

- Roll the ball in circles on the floor.

- Move the ball from left to right hands.

Differentiation
- Change the ball size.

- Work in pairs – sit back to back passing the ball to each other.

- Sit on the floor or standing up.

Idea 2 – Pancake in the Pan
The children each start with a pan and pancake (a marker and a beanbag).

- They hold the marker in their two hands like it is a pan.

- Place the beanbag in the marker and they need to then toss the pancake with the pan.

- Be sure to catch the pancake.
- How many times can they catch the pancake?

DIFFERENTIATION

- Can use hands as the pan.
- Toss and catch the pancake in pairs (start standing not too far and move further apart when it becomes easy).
- Change from beanbags to small ball.
- Bounce and catch in the pan.

BENEFITS

This develops gross motor skills, fine motor skills, throwing and catching, body awareness, spatial awareness, social skills, communication and taking turns.

AREAS THIS ACTIVITY COVERS

Expressive arts, design and creative development
Knowledge of and understanding the world
Language, literacy and communication
Personal, social and emotional development
Mathematics and numeracy

IDEA 3 – ON THE FARM

1. Set up a farm with different farm foods (coloured cones, spots or markers) scattered in an area (the field) with an entrance gate on the right and exit gate on the left side of the field.
2. Allocate an area near the exit gate where food will be stored.
3. Divide children into groups of four or five, allocating a breed of animal to each group.
4. The adult calls out an animal (that has been allocated to one of the groups) – that group runs, entering the field through the gate and collects one piece of 'food'.
5. They then exit the field, place the food on the same colour pile in an allocated area and return to the beginning.

6. Repeat for each group.

7. Once all children have had a turn, ask them to help you plant food in the field again. They will pick up one piece of food and place it around the field.

8. Progression: Repeat from point 1 with children making the sound of the animal and acting it out.

9. Once all groups have had a turn repeat point 4.

10. Progression: Repeat point 5 but tell them what coloured food they need to collect.

BENEFITS

This develops gross motor skills, fine motor skills, spatial awareness, social skills, communication, listening skills and taking turns.

AREAS THIS ACTIVITY COVERS

Expressive arts, design and creative development
Knowledge of and understanding the world
Language, literacy and communication
Personal, social and emotional development

Chapter 6

KNOWLEDGE AND UNDERSTANDING OF THE WORLD

(Including Technology, Science and Geography)

Knowledge and understanding of the world and movement and active play go hand in hand. Children do not find out about the world around them through us telling them or from books, they learn through discovering, exploring and experiencing for themselves.

Many children have little opportunity to explore different environments with their families and most of their experience of the world happens through a television screen. Spending time in forest school, or visiting the park via the local fruit and vegetable shop, not only gets children moving but also helps them to understand the world around them.

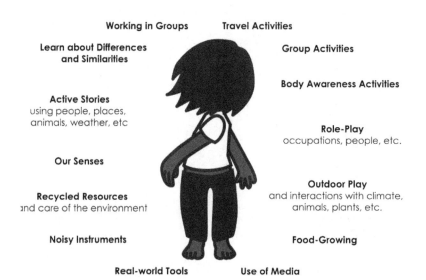

Working in Groups　Travel Activities

Learn about Differences
and Similarities

Group Activities

Body Awareness Activities

Active Stories
using people, places,
animals, weather, etc

Role-Play
occupations, people, etc.

Our Senses

Outdoor Play
and interactions with climate,
animals, plants, etc.

Recycled Resources
and care of the environment

Noisy Instruments　Food-Growing

Real-world Tools　Use of Media

HOW PHYSICAL ACTIVITY IMPACTS CHILDREN'S KNOWLEDGE AND UNDERSTANDING OF THE WORLD

When children are playing and being active they will be discovering so much about the world around them, including themselves, others, the natural world and materials they may come across.

- Activities help children to understand similarities and differences between people, places, objects, cultures and many other aspects of our world.

- Active stories and role play about different people (different occupations, countries, your neighbourhood, etc.) are an enjoyable, non-threatening way to learn about the world, locally, nationally and globally.

- Inclusion in identifying the plot and outcome of active stories or imaginative play activities allow children to use their knowledge and interests, learning about what they do and do not know.

- Activities such as creating games from 'rubbish' (boxes, bottle tops, etc.) can teach children about recycling and taking care of the environment.

- Exploring their surroundings and discovering the people in them help children develop physically; the more physically able they are, the more they can explore.

- Self-directed play is important for exploring their environment through what interests them and at a pace that is suitable for them.

- Games with noisy objects (shaking, hitting, etc.) that are either made or supplied will help children understand different sounds, levels and tones.

- Manipulating real-world tools and objects (putting a lid on a teapot, etc.) will make sense of their surroundings and support creativity.

- Manipulating and operating toys with buttons and other mechanisms not only develops their fine motor skills but will spark their early ICT (information and communication technologies) learning and skills.

- Use of media to encourage movement, e.g. CD player, activities/dances on the internet, will teach children about media and how they differ and how different types of media work.

- Children work together, use imagination and creativity to problem-solve which will help them to learn about each other and how to work in a group.

- Gardening teaches children about plants, growth and life cycles.

- Activities that include food and food growing tasks and discussions teach children about the natural world.

- Travel games (cars, bicycles, aeroplanes, etc.) will help children understand different places, how to get to them and an initial understanding of distances. It also teaches children about road safety, their local environment and the world.

- Through outdoor play children become familiar with various plants, trees, birds, small animals and minibeasts.

- Regular outdoor play helps children to learn about how the world around them changes, such as cold, hot, sunny, rainy and the seasons.

- Active stories about the weather, the seasons, day and night, animals, trees and other plants, birds, etc. make learning fun and accessible.

- Body awareness games help children learn about their body parts and how they fit together

- Children learn about their senses through active stories, movement to music, songs and games.

- Grouping activities can support science and mathematics, such as what animals eat grass, how many different types of animals eat grass? What do other animals eat?

- Aiming and throwing games can teach children about different objects, such as what material they are made from, the difference in sizes, the difference in shapes and which ones are heavier.

- Obstacle courses using natural and discarded material can help children become familiar with various materials, natural and man-made.

Role play and active stories can also help children to understand the world further afield, such as the sea, jungles, deserts, other countries and about the roles different people play in society, such as doctor, firefighter or grandfather. Learning about other places and people will help them become more tolerant and understanding of others and learn to take care of their environment. Furthermore, they will learn better and be more likely to retain the information if they are enjoying moving, being creative and using their imagination.

Much of what children learn in the early years will be the start of their discovery of science, geography and ICT.

ASPECTS OF KNOWLEDGE AND UNDERSTANDING OF THE WORLD

Animals

- Animals we know, pets, etc.

- Animals from different countries

- Minibeasts

- Land animals

- Birds

- Fish

- Life cycles (butterflies/worms/frogs)

Through movement and active play we pretend to be different animals. Creating stories about animals and their surroundings, such as a tiger in the jungle, or animals on the farm, will bring them to life and help children to learn about and understand them.

Top Tip – Use of animals in physical education lesson or structured sessions will not only stimulate children's imagination and make the activities more fun but can also help children to learn about the animal world.

Children will naturally learn about minibeasts, birds, fish, insects and other local creatures when exploring environments such as gardens, forests, parks and the seaside.

Colours

- Creating different colours
- Colours in nature

Large painting, drawing and mark making is fun and energetic. Children will naturally learn about different plants and creatures and different colours when exploring environments such as gardens, forests, parks and the seaside.

Plants

- Growing
- Seeds
- Differences and similarities
- What plants need to grow
- Where our food comes from
- Parts of plant/flower

Young children learn many things from food growing and gardening and have a great time doing so. Activities and active stories about food and food growing are an enjoyable way for children to learn about nature. When they have opportunities to explore an array of environments they will discover different plants.

Senses

- How sounds are generated in different ways
- Tones
- Loudness
- Matching sounds
- Different sights
- Different textures

- Different smells
- Different tastes

Myself

- Body parts (body awareness)
- What we need to remain healthy
- Similarities and differences between me and others
- Similarities and differences between humans and others animals

Water

- Different states and bodies of water, e.g. lakes, rivers, ice, mist
- Movement in water, e.g. waves, currents
- How objects react with water, e.g. float, sink

Shapes and Patterns

- Natural and manmade patterns
- How the world is made up of different shapes
- How different shapes fit together

Transport and Travel

- Different types of transport
- How travel affects our lives, the local area and the whole world

Our World

- Different countries
- Different cultures
- Differences and similarities
- Where we live and our family
- Local places such as our house, flat, village, town, road, church, temple

People

- Differences and similarities between boys and girls
- Uniqueness of all
- Difference and similarities of all
- Myself and other living things
- Myself and non-living things
- Different workplaces and roles people play in society

Time

- Growing up
- How time impacts on us and our lives
- How time impacts other living and non-living things
- Sequencing the passing of time (a day, a year, a lifetime, etc.)
- The past and the present
- Old and new
- Talking about significant events in our lives

Materials and their Properties

- Different natural materials, e.g. sand, clay, wood, stones
- How interaction of materials can make changes to them
- Shapes of material and how some change
- Properties of natural and manmade materials

Environment

- Changes
- Weather
- Seasons
- Recycling
- Climate change

Light and Electricity

- Different times of day
- Light and dark
- Light sources
- Different seasons and change in length of daylight
- Electricity at home, including safety
- Using and making electrical circuits

Forces

- Push
- Pull
- Throw
- Roll
- How different objects move
- How we move

Sorting

- Sorting animals, objects, people, etc. into groups

Technology

- Understanding how to operate and operating simple toys and equipment that need manipulation
- Using media such as CD players, computer music programmes, remote controls, mobile phones and cameras
- Understanding basic use of computers and programming

Children will need to develop the following skills to discover the world around them:

- express opinions and describe objects, occurrences and outcomes
- observe and explore, show curiosity and experiment
- sort, compare, group and sequence

- communicate their thoughts and listen to others
- problem-solving and decision-making
- classify and record
- predict, evaluate and reflect.

NATURAL DEVELOPMENT

Examples of how children will learn about knowledge of and understanding of the world through self-directed movement and active play in the early years include the following:

- When children are exploring the outdoor environment, they are learning about animals and bugs, plants, forces, the environment, the weather, seasons and different natural materials.

- Children learn about time, what affects growth and different plants through gardening and food growing.

- As adults we can make use of many teachable and reflective moments by asking questions that will encourage them to think about what they are experiencing.

- Children can discover many different worlds, cultures, people and places through role play and active stories. Active stories can be created spontaneously using their imagination or can be an extension of subjects you have been exploring. Active stories and role play will also give children the opportunity to discover the differences and similarities between themselves and others and also to discover their impact on the environment. This will make more sense than learning from books. Children can also discover more about themselves and time through active stories based on their lives, from babies, to current times, to when they will be adults.

- There are many rhymes about subjects such as our body parts, the world and animals that help children learn about the world around them and themselves. Make them big and energetic.

- Simple trips such as going to the park or to the local shops will help children to get a sense of the local area and the diversity within it. They will be able to discover different plants, people, textures, buildings and shops. In many areas they will also discover people from different countries and cultures.

- Visiting farms, zoos, etc., children will learn about animals, their differences and similarities, where they live, what they eat, how we interact with them.

- When children create constructions out of boxes and other recycled household goods they will discover how to manipulate materials and how objects and materials fit together.

- Creating imaginative objects out of recycled and natural objects and materials will help children to learn about how we can take care of our environment by recycling and taking care of what and how much we use.

- Using real-world tools and other real objects such as china, sewing kits and knives for cooking helps children to connect with what really happens around them.

- Children can learn how water can turn into different forms and when mixed with other materials can change into something else, e.g. mist, ponds, ice, mud.

- Through water play they can discover how some objects float and others sink.

- Children can learn how combining natural materials can change them, such as sand and water creating mud or flour, water and salt creating playdough.

Through all these activities, children will develop understanding of the world around them and begin to learn the basics of science, geography and history. Everything we learn is based on what we already know so the more we discover through exploration and joy in the early years, the more we will learn and discover as we grow older.

PHYSICAL ACTIVITY IDEAS

Here is an outline of some of the types of activities that support learning in this area:

- active stories
- active rhymes

- action songs
- gardening and food growing
- healthy eating and cooking/food preparation
- local area and the world – going for walks, map making
- body awareness activities
- my senses activities
- cultural songs, dances, stories and games
- going on holiday or an adventure
- building and construction
- exploring us – similarities and differences
- activities that incorporate road safety,
  water safety and anti-bullying
- activities that incorporate colours, patterns and shapes
- treasure and scavenger hunts
- weighing, measuring and comparing sizes
- bubbles, mud, water play
- simple science – exploring and experiments
- simple geography – beach, mountains,
  weather, etc. who has visited where?

Ideas

Activities from Chapter 11 that support this area of learning include the following activities:

* Active Alphabets
* Aim and Score
* Animal Obstacle Courses
* Ball Stop
* Bigger! 'Head shoulders knees and toes'
* Cats and Rabbits
* Cone Catches
* Colours
* Mini Yo! (or other yoga-based resources)
* Monkey Madness

* Movement to Music and Dances Ideas
* Musical Statue Champions
  * In pairs
  * Feather Dance
  * Listen and Move
  * Ribbon Dance
  * Dancing Stories
* Musical Groups
* Slow Mo
* Superheroes to the rescue
* the Boat (Mini Yo! or other yoga-based cards)

Mini Moves

Children need to develop many physical skills when they are young to prepare them for sports, physical education and cognitive learning. Many of these skills can be developed naturally through children playing and moving for a large part of each day. However, even the most active children need support from those who care for them to ensure they are developing and are equipped with all the skills they need.

Mini Moves is a pack of 18 brightly coloured cards, each covering a particular physical skill. The cards have the name of the skill and an image of the skill being performed on one side and an explanation of how the skill is performed, with various activity idea suggestions, on the other side. There are many more than the 18 physical skills that young children need to be exposed to and to develop (see Chapter 2), however the pack is a great place to start for busy teachers and early years practitioners. All that you will require are two to four of the cards. These can be incorporated into activities children already know and love, can be used to create an active story or combined to make a series of activities.

Planning around Skills

Children who are left to their own devices will develop; however, if their abilities are challenged and if they are encouraged to try new activities and skills they will not only develop more, but also develop a wider range of abilities. A list of physical skills that young children need to develop was initially identified by the PEPA (Physical Education Physical Activity)

Group, Birmingham City Council and other professionals and has since been added to and amended by me and other practitioners. The full list of early years physical skills can be found in Chapter 2. These early years skills are a precursor to the Fundamental Movement Skills that children need to become proficient in, in order to take part in sports and more complex games and activities when they are older.

An effective way to ensure children develop all the skills is to plan around them for physical education lessons. Select three or four skills each week and plan a different activity each day that incorporate these skills. Other skills can be included in the activities, but should not be the focus. Activity ideas include active stories, dancing and movement to music, obstacle courses, Simon Says, Traffic Light game, etc. There are also ideas in Chapter 11.

If an activity is planned with a specific outcome, it is potentially more successful for both the children and the practitioner. Planning around specific skills help:

- practitioners focus on observing and assessing specific skills
- practitioners identify skills where children require additional support
- practitioners develop new activities on a regular basis
- children to develop more and develop a wider variety of skills.

Top Tip – Inform parents of the skills that will be used each week and encourage them to use them at home. Provide them with ideas that they can use at home and inform them of the activities you find effective at your school or setting.

The Mini Moves cards can also be used during child-directed play by placing them in the outdoor area. Children can then try them out as and when they choose. If they have been exposed to enjoyable activities based on the skills, they will be more likely to keep trying out the skills.[1]

---

1 You can find out more about the Mini Moves resource at www.binspireduk.co.uk/ resources.

Shared Practice

Where in the World?

By Dan Winch

I have been teaching at Ballard School for 12 years, initially as an NQT and now as Head of Pre-Prep Physical Education, teaching from Kindergarten 1 (2 years old) to Year 11 (16 years old). I also lead and host the annual Independent Schools Association, London West Pre-Prep Sports Festival.

This is a basic geography activity for children in Key Stage 1 or can be simplified for younger children. It can obviously be adapted for children in other countries, with discussions about that particular country.

In an active area, (a sports hall is good or a coned large square 15m x 15m), pupils play a north, south, east, west game with the teacher pointing to the compass directions.

Progression 1
The teacher no longer points to the directions but says the compass direction. This encourages memory skills.

Progression 2
The next step is adding north east, north west, south west, south east. This task begins with pointing and voice and quickly progresses to just using your voice.

Progression 3
Pupils are given a place in Britain that is in the north, a place in the east, west and south. Pupils have to remember where the places are. There is no pointing now.

Progression 4
The teacher adds more places each time so pupils have to remember more places.

Progression 5
Pupils then go away and come back to the next lesson with places in Britain that they have found on the British map. The game is then played again with the pupils' suggestions.

These activities can be completed for five minutes at the start of a series of lessons and progress with each lesson.

Benefits

Area of learning: geography (knowledge of and understanding the world), listening, problem-solving, language and communication.

Chapter 7

EXPRESSIVE ARTS, DESIGN AND CREATIVE DEVELOPMENT

Expressive arts, design and creative development is all about children expressing themselves when moving to music and dancing, singing, creating and playing music, experimenting with various materials, colours, textures, forms and shape as well as design and mark making. So much of this will be experienced when children are on the move, in structured sessions and lessons, in play, inside and outside. Yes, children can sit down to create art and crafts but why keep it small and why keep them still when they could use their whole body to express themselves?

Large Painting

Movement to Music

Active Rhymes

Action Songs

Colour & Space Activities

Self-expression
through movement
& creativity

Use of Patterns
and Shapes

Repetition of Actions

Music and
Instrument Creation

Dance Basics
such as travel, turn,
jump, gesture,
stand still and fall

Building & Construction
using creativity and
imagination

Noisy Instruments

Active Stories

Use of Natural Materials

Open-Ended Resources

Drawing to Music

HOW PHYSICAL ACTIVITY IMPACTS CHILDREN'S DEVELOPMENT OF EXPRESSIVE ARTS, DESIGN AND CREATIVE DEVELOPMENT

Children will develop their creativity, rhythm, self-expression and understanding of themselves, including their thoughts, feelings and ideas through movement and active play.

- Gross motor activities underpin the development of fine motor skills.

- Children will naturally develop their fine motor skills when exploring the environment.

- Dance and movement to music should make up a large part of physical education lessons and daily activities in the early years.

- Learning rhythm through movement to music and active rhymes will teach children about dance and song.

- Through different movements, such as high for loud and low for soft, tiptoe for high pitch and stomp for low pitch, children will develop an understanding of the changes in music.

- The use of colour and space in activities will teach children about design and use of media.

- Children copy movements role-modelled by adults during physical education lessons and activities led by adults.

- Children express feelings and emotions through movements, gestures and other activities.

- Children should receive the opportunity to create images and move in ways they choose, allowing them to express themselves.

- Imitation of actions performed by adults, such as clapping, waving, etc., will lead to children learning to perform various actions themselves. Performing actions in a repetitive manner will teach children about rhythm and dance.

- Develop dance sequences based on stories or on dance basics (travel, jump, turn, gesture, pause/still and fall). Initially this should be led by adults, but as children develop in their abilities and skill levels they can be tasked to create their own dance sequences.

- Give children the opportunity to move instruments, creating sounds. They can make their own instruments from resources found around the house, the outdoors and by recycling objects that would normally be discarded.

- Building and construction engages creativity and imagination as well as innovation and invention.

- Role-play games which include imagination and fact allow children to use their knowledge and ideas.

- Active stories will encourage children to move in different ways whilst using their imagination.

- Giving children opportunities to make up stories, rhymes, movements to music allows them to use their imagination and creativity.

- Children can create art and develop design techniques outdoors using natural materials or a combination of natural materials and resources provided.

- Provide a wide variety of construction materials, textiles and other objects to allow children to use their imagination to create and build.

- When provided with a variety of materials, children will learn to design and construct creatively.

- Large painting, design and mark making is a good starting point for young children who have not yet refined their fine motor skills. Many children will respond positively to this rather than sitting down and focusing on a small area. Add music and you will not only make the experience more enjoyable but children will gain another level of creativity and expression.

- Use of open-ended resources (resources that do not have one specific use and can be used in many different ways) will stimulate creativity and imagination.

Basing activities in the early years on active stories and imagination will create more engaging and enjoyable experiences for young children. The use of music will also enhance many activities and encourage self-expression, sometimes a little too much!

Top Tip – Music can enhance many activities and encourage children to move more. Always be armed with music when you want to get children moving!

Not only does movement and active play underpin self-expression and imagination but gross motor development underpins fine motor skills. As discussed in Chapter 4, the building blocks of fine motor skills are stability of the body, sensation, and bilateral co-ordination, which are developed through gross motor opportunities. It is important for those who work with young children to be aware of this as many children struggle with fine motor tasks due to lack of movement and active play opportunities.

ASPECTS OF EXPRESSIVE ARTS, DESIGN AND CREATIVE DEVELOPMENT

Expressive Arts, Design and Creative Development can be divided into three sections.

Art, Craft and Design

Children will explore different media, resources, colours and patterns, using their memory, senses, observational skills, critical thinking, invention and imagination to create two-dimensional images and three-dimensional structures.

When people think of arts and crafts they usually associate them with sitting at a table or on the ground, drawing, sticking, painting, cutting and marking. However, so much can be done on a large scale, inside and outside, using different body parts and this can require gross motor skills, not only fine motor skills.

Stories and Imaginative Play

So much of what children do naturally involves their imagination and imaginative play. Taking the lead from children and understanding how they learn will enable you to help them to engage and develop in the ways they should.

Active stories are not only engaging and enjoyable for young children but can also encourage them to create their own stories and storylines. This, along with role play, is the start of drama, teaching children to act out various roles and subject matter.

It is also a lot easier for a child to grasp a concept or new idea if they learn through the use of their imagination. Children will be able to explore different feelings and emotions and other areas of their lives through many activities that incorporate imagination.

Music, Dance and Movement to Music

Even before babies can stand, when music is played you will find them moving to it. Making music, singing action songs and reciting active rhymes will positively impact children's physical and language skills. They are also important for building sequencing skills.

Allowing children to freely move to music allows them to express themselves with their whole body. Some children, and adults, will find this difficult and will respond better to structured movement to music activities, where they follow instructions or mimic movements. Children can learn to combine various movements to create movement patterns and can also learn to work in pairs and groups and, as they get older, should be given the opportunity to create their own movement patters, using the basic dance skills of travel, turn, jump, gesture, still and fall.

Top Tip – As young children enjoy stories and imaginative play, stories and activities can also be extended into movement to music activities. Involve children in determining moves or the storyline to allow the use of their creative thinking.

THE IMPORTANCE OF CREATIVITY

When children are creative they:

- think about and communicate ideas symbolically
- learn what they can and cannot do
- set challenges for themselves, problem-solve and try new things
- build on previous experiences
- develop a better understanding of materials and objects in their environment

- discover how to make things out of basic material and media

- take chances and discover new things

- learn about the world around them

- become able to express their opinions, thoughts and ideas

- learn to persevere. When children aim to create something new, they will, no doubt, make some mistakes. If they really want to achieve what they set out to do they will need to think critically, problem-solve and try again. If they do persevere, they will be more likely to continue to try new things and be open to new experiences.

- develop their language and communication skills, especially through active stories, rhymes and songs and engaging in role play and other cooperative play

- develop their social skills and confidence, as well as improve their reading and mathematical skills

- develop creative thinking which is necessary for other areas of learning such as science and mathematics

- develop intellectual processes that allow them to develop or understand ideas and concepts in many areas of life.

There is so much pressure on those who work with young children to provide completed work on a regular basis that the process, and what children learn and discover through creative play, is not always valued. It might take a few attempts for children to achieve what they set out to do but the fact that they persevered, thought critically, problem-solved and confronted the task with a creative mind will be a huge learning process for that child.

Open-ended play and resources will help to develop children's creativity, allowing and encouraging them to use their imagination, try something new, experiment and explore. When purchasing resources and toys always think about whether children can use the toy in different ways, just using a little imagination. Collecting recycled objects (obviously ones that are hygienic and safe) can be just as good, if not better, than some of those expensive resources that catch your eye.

Top Tip – Provide children with the opportunity to play with no resources or equipment, especially when outdoors. This will encourage them to use their imagination and creativity, to use what is in the environment and turn it into anything they wish. Be careful not to prompt them as they could then be steered away from critical thinking, creativity and innovation.

NATURAL DEVELOPMENT

Examples of how children will learn about expressive arts, design and develop creatively through self-directed movement and active play in the early years:

- Children will discover different patterns and marks in the outdoor environment and they will discover patterns and marks that they make themselves in mud and sand.

- Children will build structures and dens, using their imagination and creativity to turn them into castles, dragon's dens, towers, ships, etc. They will learn how to use different materials to build, how malleable and inflexible materials fit together and use of materials and objects to decorate their den.

- Using natural objects, such as leaves, feathers, sticks and flowers, children might be inclined to create beautiful pictures and patterns.

- You might find children running around the outdoor area in strange outfits pretending to be a superhero, a butterfly or an aeroplane, expressing themselves through imaginative play. They might also be dressing up like a mummy or daddy and running around pushing baby in a pushchair.

- Rhymes and songs with actions and movements are always favourites for young children. The repetition of rhymes and songs help children to master new skills and also explore the world.

- If children have access to spray bottles, paint brushes, rollers and a source of water, you will often find them painting just about anything outside. This will help them develop their creativity whilst developing fine and gross motor skills.

- When children have access to recycled objects they really get to use their imagination and creativity, as these objects provide great open-ended activities. You will find them making space ships, their superhero lair or a bridge over the magic lake, allowing them to play with their interests in mind.

- Children will create and build when they have access to real-world tools, sawing, nailing and whittling wood.

- Mud is wonderfully open-ended, easy to manipulate, change and work with and children can be really creative with this messy substance. Team a child up with mud and those brain cells of theirs will spark. You will find them creating mud cakes, patterns and building castles.

PHYSICAL ACTIVITY IDEAS

Physical activities that support expressive arts, design and creative development are endless. Following is an outline of some of the types of activities that support learning in this area:

- movement to music
- active rhymes
- active stories
- action songs
- creating and playing instruments
- use of streamers and ribbons
- painting with water
- painting and drawing to music
- creating collages (from natural and man-made materials)
- large painting and mark making
- 3D models with objects and materials found outdoors
- role play
- junk modelling
- superhero activities
- use of body parts, body-awareness activities.

Ideas

Activities from Chapter 11 that support this area of learning include the following activities:

* Active Alphabets
* Active Cube
* Active Stories
* Animal Obstacle Courses
* Ball Stop
* Bigger! 'Head shoulders knees and toes'
* Big Nursery Rhymes
* Cats and Rabbits
* Cone Catches
* Colours
* Magic Rocks and the Giant (Hide the Spot!)
* Mini Yo! (or other yoga-based resources)
* Monkey Madness
* Movement to Music and Dances Ideas
  * Musical Statue Champions
  * In pairs
  * Feather Dance
  * Listen and Move
  * Ribbon Dance
  * Dancing Stories
* Musical Groups
* Paper Fortune Teller
* Props
* Shadows
* Slow Mo
* Superheroes to the Rescue
* The Boat (Mini Yo! or other yoga-based cards)

Shared Practice

Tennis Ball Painting

By Karen Lesley Gaskill

I have worked in Foundation Stage as a Teaching Assistant for a total of around 25 years, taking a break to have my own children and returning later. My role in school has changed and I am now the Inclusion Manager, supporting the families around Health, Safeguarding, and so much more.

Resources

Large paper

Instructions

- Roll out a large piece of paper, I used to use the back of a wall paper roll.
- A child sits at each end of the paper.
- One has a bowl of paint with a tennis ball in it.
- The first child rolls the ball to the second child sitting on the other end of the paper.
- The second child then rolls the ball back.
- This continues for a few rolls, then they swap so that the second child has the bowl with paint in.

They loved it; I would have a queue waiting!

Benefits

I found it covered a range of learning areas and benefits:

- PSED – turn taking, working together, eye contact.
- Numeracy – counting, colours.
- Language and Communication – initiating communication, listening.
- Physical – fine motor, gross motor if using bigger balls.

Chapter 8

SPIRITUAL, MORAL, SOCIAL AND CULTURAL (SMSC) DEVELOPMENT

Spiritual, Moral, Social and Cultural Development should underpin a school or early years setting's values and ethos. The four areas of SMSC will therefore be learnt and developed throughout a child's day. Children learn these values through all areas of learning and subjects and through the ethos of their place of learning and care.

For children to live full and active lives and to grow into well-rounded adults they do not just need to develop physically and academically. They also need to establish strong morals and values, learn about positive relationships and belonging in society, right from wrong and being good to others, other living beings and themselves. They also need to developing a sense of self, understanding their abilities and fulfilling their potential.

Irrespective of whether children live in a country where SMSC Development or something similar is part of their curriculum, it is important for us all to develop a set of morals and values with guidance from those who care for us.

Build Self-worth & Confidence
through creative play

Develop a Sense of Belonging
through role play and active stories

Learn about the World
by acting out
active stories

Build a Respect for Nature
by playing outdoors

Social Skill Development
by working in pairs
and groups

Develop Morals & Values
through play and
activities

**Learn about
Health & Well-being**
through action songs and
active stories

Learn Respect for Others
by interacting and playing
with others

Experience Other Cultures
through cultural activities
and dances

**Learn about Diversity
and Acceptance**
through activities and playing
with other children

Anti-Bullying Activities   **Road-Safety Activities**

HOW PHYSICAL ACTIVITIES IMPACT CHILDREN'S SPIRITUAL, MORAL, SOCIAL AND CULTURAL DEVELOPMENT

Physical activities such as active stories, action songs and group games help children to explore right from wrong, how they fit into society and to respect themselves and the world around them.

Spiritual Development

- When children are being creative, building a den, creating and acting out an active story or moving to music, they will learn about their abilities, what they can and cannot do; and when they achieve what they set out to do, they develop a sense of self-worth and confidence. Remember not always to tell them how well they have done, let them identify their own achievements.

- Role play, active stories and various games help children to understand the world around them and how they fit into the world.

- Active stories can be based on topics of your choice, encouraging children to be active, while learning about the world around them.

- When children are exploring the outdoors, using recycled material to build with, building minibeast dens or walking next to a river, they learn about respecting the environment and other living creatures.

Moral Development

- Children learn many social and emotional skills when being active and playing in groups and pairs. They learn social skills, including turn taking, respect, winning, loosing, following rules and empathy. These are skills young children cannot be taught, but need to discover and learn about through experience.

- As children grow older, they will find it easier to understand and implement good moral values if they have been exposed to these values through play and activities at a younger age.

Social Development

- At first, babies and young children prefer to play on their own and need to be taught about sharing and taking turns. Through games and fun activities, children learn to respect others, identify their role in a group and, if given the opportunity, discover their voice in their community.

- When playing in a pair or group, children will learn that if they work together they can achieve a common goal.

- They learn to play to each other's strengths and to exploit the weakness of an 'opponent' in order to succeed in competition.

- Lack of spatial awareness, perhaps through little opportunity to be active when children are young or through medical conditions, can have a negative impact on children's social skills, often making them unpopular or lead to them finding it hard to fit in.

- Children learn about their own health and well-being through activities, songs, active stories and role play.

- Risk taking is an important part of physical development and having many opportunities to push themselves in a safe and secure environment will teach children about risk management, their abilities and setting themselves challenges.

Cultural Development

- Children can play games, experience active stories and dance to music that reflect different cultures.

- Role play teaches children about the world around them and to respect differences.

- Physical activities and games teach children about their differences and similarities.

- Children and adults alike need to learn about, understand, develop their knowledge and accept difference and diversity. Role play, active stories, active rhymes and many games are a non-threatening way to teach children about others.

- Group games and activities teach young children about the dynamics of healthy relationships.

- Most young children naturally understand the concepts of justice, peace and forgiveness; however, through active play children can learn to express their opinions and learn to respect others' opinions.

- Subjects such as anti-bullying and road safety awareness can be part of games, physical activities and songs, providing children with important knowledge in an enjoyable manner. If they enjoy learning they will most likely retain the information.

Spiritual

Children learn about themselves, their strengths and weaknesses, values, meaning and purpose through creativity and imagination. Children explore the world around them and themselves, making sense of life, their beliefs and creating perspective of the non-materialistic aspects of life.

Moral

Children learn to understand the difference between right and wrong, being good to others and respecting rules and laws. They discover how their behaviour and choices can affect them and those around them, understand consequences and learn about forgiving themselves and others. Children should have the right to air disagreements and understand that not everyone has the same opinions.

Social

Children learn about respecting others, positive relationships, their roles and responsibilities as part of a local or global community, or family, and the ability to interact with others in a positive manner. Young children, in particular, need to understand that their will and opinion might not always be best for the common good. The development of social skills in young children can have a profound impact on their success as adults, personally and in a work environment.

Cultural

Children develop an understanding of different cultures, and respect and accept diversity. They will learn about their own culture and other cultures and to celebrate similarities and differences.

Young children need to learn how to interact with others in a group environment and also need to learn to understand their emotions. Rather than trying (and probably failing!) to explain these skills to them, give them the opportunity and they will learn through interacting with others. Many adult- and child-initiated group-based activities will give children the opportunity to explore and discover their place in society and how they can positively contribute to it.

Children are Individuals

Every child is different and has specific interests, unique ways in which they are learning, and will have had an array of different experiences. Adults therefore need to develop strategies to help all children succeed, bearing in mind that:

- some children may learn by trial and error, whereas other children will learn by watching others before trying something new themselves

- some children need step-by-step instructions demonstrated with guidance

- some may find it easier to perform a skill outside; other children might feel more secure inside

- some may be better able to learn from another child rather than from an adult.

TEMPERAMENT

Temperament is our nature and affects how we behave. The way children react to different situations is affected by their temperament. Some are shy and cautious, whereas others will be enthusiastic and keen to try new activities.

INTERESTS

Children have unique interests which motivate them to learn. Used effectively, these interests can provide a great tool to assist learning. If a child is reluctant to engage, their interests can be used to help them interact with others, be more active and have more rewarding learning experiences.

CULTURE

The culture of a child has an impact on the way they think, talk, express and feel about personal space. Culture is not only related to their nationality or religion, but also to the beliefs, values and morals of their family. There are cultures, for example, where personal space is prized highly, and others where contact is considered the norm. Personal space, or the lack of it, can also be learnt through the culture of an individual family.

LEARNING STYLES

We do not all learn in the same way, different styles work best for different children, and adults. The three main styles of learning are auditory, visual and kinasthetic.

Auditory Learners

Auditory learners learn best through sounds and words. They can easily follow instructions and explanations.

Visual Learners

These children learn best by observing and tend to think in images or pictures. Visual learners learn best when they are shown how to do things.

Kinaesthetic Learners

These are children who learn best by moving. They are usually coordinated and confident movers. Kinaesthetic learners need to move to learn and understand.

LIFE EXPERIENCES

Experiences and circumstances in life play a role in a child's ability to learn. It is important to find out as much about the child from their family in order to 'paint a picture' of them. They may learn differently if they are the oldest child of a large family, or if they are an only child. Their ability to learn may also be affected if they have recently been, or are currently, going through a traumatic experience, such as divorce, death of a loved one or moving countries.

SPECIAL NEEDS

If a child is gifted or disabled, it is important to remember that this is only one aspect of the child, not the whole child; all should be seen as individuals.

CHILDREN WITH DISABILITIES

It is always important to work with specialists, and your approach to working with any child should be based on the same principle – identify the child's strengths and weaknesses and plan what changes and adjustments can be made to support the child to learn. Always focus on what children are able to do and build on that. If it is possible to identify their 'developmental age' then it is easy to plan appropriate activities for them based on the abilities of children of that age.

Ultimately, our aim for disabled children should be the same as for any other child. Yes, it can be a greater challenge but it is important for all children to be engaged and active and they should be offered an environment and opportunities that will enhance their potential and develop their abilities through enriching experiences.

PHYSICAL ACTIVITY IDEAS

All physical activities will support learning in this area. Spiritual, Moral, Social and Cultural development occurs throughout the day and through just about everything children do with others and on their own. It is the role of the adult to help children make sense of this and what better way than through enjoyable physical activities and play?

Here is a list of some activities from Chapter 11 that support learning in this area:

* Active Cube
* Active Stories
* Aim and Score
* Beanbag Relay Races
* Big Nursery Rhymes
* Cats and Rabbits
* Cone Catches
* Colours
* Magic Rocks and the Giant
* Mini Yo!
* Monkey Madness
* Dancing Stories
* Musical Groups
* Shadows
* Superheroes to the Rescue

Chapter 9

RISK TAKING AND RISKY PLAY

Challenges and risk taking are important for children to develop physically, socially, and even cognitively. Though the outdoors offers many opportunities for this, risk taking can take place anywhere that a child needs to push themselves or try something new. Children will be more willing to take risks and attempt new challenges if they feel they are supported by the adults who care for them and are in a safe and secure environment. They also need to learn about being safe, as well as respecting the environment and people around them.

Play and risk go hand-in-hand. If we are to truly value play then we must also value risk.[1]

THE IMPORTANCE OF RISK TAKING

Children develop physically, cognitively and emotionally through risk taking. The process of learning and developing involves trying new things that are slightly out of our reach and persevering until we reach them.

Risk taking in a controlled environment will help children to make better decisions when they are not within the safety of a school or early years setting. If children are not exposed to risk taking in a safe environment they are exposed to another kind of danger: they may never learn to assess risk and their own ability. Some children may become timid, never taking valuable risks, whereas others may make foolhardy decisions and potentially come to harm.

Risk taking not only helps children to grow and develop but also encourages children to be creative, develop their social skills as well as playing a part in the development of resilience. If a child learns

---

1 Play England (2008) 'Managing risk in play provision: A position statement.' Available at www.playengland.org.uk/resource/managing-risk-in-play-provision-a-position-statement, accessed on 19 December 2016.

to take chances, fails and tries again, they will learn to face many challenges and barriers in their lives with a positive outlook.

WHAT IS RISKY PLAY?

Norwegian researcher, Hansen Sandseter,[2] identified what risky play looks like:

- heights – play with heights where children can be at risk of falling and possibly hurting themselves

- speed – play at high speed where children can lose control which may lead to them colliding with others or into other objects

- tools – play with harmful tools where if children are not taught safety they can be harmed by them

- elements – play near dangerous elements where there may be a possibility of injury from the elements or they may fall into, such as a river

- rough and tumble – rough and tumble play where children can be harmed by each other

- disappear/get lost – play where children can disappear/get lost and possibly come to harm due to lack of adult supervision and care.

RISK VS. BENEFIT OF RISKY PLAY

When caring for young children you will need to be aware of:

- the difference between acceptable or good, and unacceptable or bad risk taking

- the balance between risk and benefits

- when to support children and when to allow them to make their own decisions and judgements

- using your own knowledge and judgement to support beneficial risk taking.

---

2 Hansen Sandseter, E.B. (2007) 'Categorising risky play: How can we identify risk-taking in children's play?' *European Early Childhood Education Research Journal 15*, 2, 237–252.

- how to use space and resources to encourage positive risk taking.

You can support and maximise the benefits of risky play by:

- developing your knowledge and confidence to provide positive risk taking, as this involves a level of personal, yet informed, judgement

- communicating correctly with children who are engaged in risky play:

  - ask children questions rather than tell them to do something. This will help them to problem-solve and learn to understand their own abilities.

  - when they are deep in concentration, attempting a challenging task, such as climbing a tree or crossing a river from stone to stone, try to communicate with them only when necessary as this can distract them from the task at hand.

- providing a safe, secure environment, which includes their relationship with you, to encourage children to push themselves

- informing and communicating with parents about your risk taking policy and explaining why it is important.

Bad Risks and Hazards

Bad risks and hazards are those that are difficult or impossible for children to assess for themselves, and that have no obvious benefits. According to Play England, these hazards can include sharp edges on equipment or points on equipment and resources, structures that are weak and may collapse, and items that can trap children's heads or fingers or other appendages.

Assessing the Risk-Benefit

Risk assessment evidences that you have identified and eliminated unacceptable risk to children and allowed for acceptable risk as opposed to eliminating all risk. According to the Managing Risk in Play Provision Play Safety Forum statement, there are three factors central to determining whether or not the risk is acceptable:

- the likelihood of coming to harm

- the severity of that harm
- the benefits, rewards or outcomes of the activity.

When considering the safety of an environment, always consider legal requirements as well as acceptable risks. Consider where the risks will be and then what measures you can put in place to minimise the risks, for example, falls from climbing equipment are possible, however the possibility of coming to harm will be reduced if hazards such as windows and sharp objects are nowhere near the equipment.

Top Tip – If children fall from equipment, they learn in a safe environment how to fall, how to get up and start over and also learn to identify their own ability better. It is obviously important to ensure that the risk of them coming to harm is very minimal by completing a risk assessment of the area and equipment.

SELF-REGULATION

Self-regulation is defined as the ability to identify and control our own behaviour, emotions, and thinking, and to amend them to allow us to respond appropriately to various situations. Exposure to challenging situations teaches children perseverance, patience and an understanding of themselves. Self-regulation is usually referred to with regards to emotions and behaviour; however, self-regulation can be learnt through risk taking and challenges and can be a useful skill when children are being physically active.

ADULT SUPPORT

Children will find challenges themselves and attempt to take risks on their own terms. It is worth keeping in mind that some will be thrill seekers and might try to challenge themselves far beyond their ability, whereas others might be fearful and give up too easily, risking missing out on important development.

It is more valuable for children to learn about their own ability, how to judge risk and understand how to avert danger, rather than us doing it all for them. Children will learn this in a supportive and safe environment through experience. It is a delicate balance the adult must maintain between inhibiting development by playing it too safe on the one hand, and putting the child in danger through unsafe risk on the other.

In order to help children to assess their own risk and ability it is not necessary for adults to always be with children when they are trying new things or pushing themselves, though it is important to keep a watchful eye and provide support when needed. If you feel a child is pushing themselves too far then it might be helpful to ask them question such as 'Look down and see where you are. Do you feel happy to be that high?' 'Do you want to try putting your foot on that block first before placing it on the higher block?'. If a child is struggling with something but just needs a little support to complete a task, then it is of course worth stepping in to prevent them from giving up – just give them a chance to figure it out first.

In the same way that children need to take risks, adults need to be confident in their own knowledge in order to also take a risk. If you do not feel totally confident, it is worth taking small steps towards full risk taking, e.g. use your common sense and start cautiously and once you feel confident look to allow riskier opportunity.

Top Tip – If you do not feel comfortable with allowing children to take risks, do so in increments. Start by allowing them to take small risks and add to that slowly but surely. It could be so much easier to remain in your comfort zone, but that would not provide the opportunities children need and deserve.

CHALLENGES

If a child does not challenge themselves, they will not develop to their full potential.

Allow children to find their own challenges. Sometimes set up small challenges to encourage reluctant children to push themselves. Do not put them in situations that they are not able to get into and out of themselves. Keep an eye out for 'teachable moments' where you can maximise children's learning through simple questions or dialogue that will get them thinking.

PARENTS AND CARERS

One of the biggest issues with risk taking is being accused, or the fear of being accused, by parents and carers that children have not been well looked after. It is therefore important to be explicit with parents and carers regarding the benefits of risk taking and what is and is not acceptable in your setting or school.

- Include information about risk taking in your physical education policy and make this clear to parents and carers.

- Educate parents and carers and encourage risk taking at home, offer suggestions and ideas.

- It is important to have confidence in our risk taking practice and not be influenced by parent and carers opposing opinions. Changing good practice due to one or two parents or carers can deprive children of the opportunities that they need.

Top Tip – If you educate, inform and include parents and carers in your risk taking practice and they still oppose, they have the right to move their child elsewhere. A threat from one parent or carer should not impact all the children in your care.

RISK AND ADDITIONAL NEEDS

It is even more important that children with disabilities are provided the opportunity to take risks. They may not have the freedom and be able to make as many choices as able-bodied children and often have many things done for them in everyday life due to safety or sometimes because it is easier for those who care for them.

Children with physical disabilities are not always able to seek out their own challenges so it is important to enable them to do so. Take them to the climbing equipment, they might only be able to pull themselves up one rung; however, the sense of achievement could be the same, if not greater, than the able-bodied child who reached the top!

AN ENVIRONMENT THAT ENABLES RISK TAKING AND RISKY PLAY

Things to Jump Off
Rocks, logs, tires, etc.

Swinging ladders

Slides

Swings

Changes in Height

Swing Bridges

Dens and Secluded Places

Climbing Structures
Trees, plants climbing equipment,
stairs and ladders,
climbing walls, fences,
movable objects such as tables

Structures for Balance
Tires, logs, low string
bridges, structures built
with loose equipment

Flat Surfaces
that allow rough and tumble
play, cycling, running, etc.

Uneven Surfaces
Rocky, uneven lawn surfaces,
overgrown areas,
stepping stones/stumps, etc.

Real World Tools
(such as hammers, knives
for cooking, china, etc.)

Slopes
for running,
cycling, rolling down

**Freedom to Engage in
Activities of Own Choice**

**Natural Environment
and Natural Resources**

EQUIPMENT
Climbing Equipment/Trees

- Do not touch children when they are climbing, if they cannot climb unaided then they should not climb higher. This will allow them to climb as high as they are capable and can prevent them from getting stuck or being unsafe. Children are more likely to fall when being held by an adult than if they are climbing on their own.

- Find a balance between leaving children to get on with the task unaided and providing verbal or physical support.

- Ask children questions about how they feel they are progressing rather than telling them how they are doing. This develops self-regulation and confidence in their own ability.

- Allow them to concentrate, avoiding speaking to them unnecessarily (telling them to be careful or watch what they are doing will distract them and could lead to them falling or hurting themselves).

- Give children the opportunity to make their own low climbing structures (from wood, tyres, blocks, small tables, etc.). Discuss safety with them.

- When children are attempting to climb structures which are slightly unsteady, ask them to think about whether they are safe and what they could do to make it safer or easier to climb.

Real-world Tools

Let children use real china, building tools, sewing kits and knives for cooking. It is important to learn to trust them and, if you teach them about safety, there will be a small risk of breakage and accidents. Put into place safety measures for example, let children use the china over carpeted areas at first, model how to carry china safely with two hands, give them blunt knives and ask them to cut easy foods such as bananas. Be sure to be relaxed about any breakages and accidents.

Using real-world tools is very beneficial for children and supports:

- the development of muscles in hands and arms as well as better control over these muscles

- fine motor development when holding a nail to be hammered in; it doesn't take long for them to learn to keep their fingers out of the way of the hammer

- better hand-eye coordination

- children to learn about the difference in force when using these tools, rather than always using plastic tools

- confidence in themselves as they are trusted to use the same implements as adults. If children are not given real-world tools and objects to use they will be aware that they are using different implements to adults. Allowing them to use real-world tools that are used by adults instils a great sense of confidence

- independence and self-discipline. Being given opportunities to use real-world tools and learn about safe handling of them will lead to them being trusted with more fragile and 'dangerous' objects, leading to faster development of gross and fine motor skills.

Top Tip – Introduce using breakables and real-world objects one step at a time so children understand the risk and how to do things independently with a minimum of breakage and injury. Be sure to give clear instructions about their safe use. Remember that young children can only follow small amounts of instruction at a time. Role modelling is also necessary for most children.

Building and Construction

- Place a selection of equipment and recycled objects in the outdoor area that allows children to build their own structures and also encourages the use of natural materials (rocks, wood, etc.) for building.

- Allow them to complete as much as they can without your assistance; do be on hand to guide when it appears it has become too challenging or if you feel the risk of harm is high (bad risk).

- Teach them to be safe by asking questions about the safety of the structure they are about to climb or the object they have built.

TEACHABLE MOMENTS THROUGH RISK TAKING

When children are experimenting, being creative and taking risks, adults will often find they are presented with great opportunities to support the development of the child's thinking and problem-solving skills if they work with the child rather than just instructing them as to what they should do. Consider the situation described below and think about how you could support Sophie to take appropriate risks to maximise the potential for learning and developing confidence.

Sophie Builds a Bridge

Sophie has made a bridge with a piece of wood and two tyres that are too far apart for the wood to be sturdy. You can tell it is rather wobbly and might not be sturdy enough to hold her weight, but can she? What do you do?

Allow Sophie the opportunity to test the structure and to realise for herself that she has not chosen suitable material or that the bridge needs to be changed slightly to make it sturdy. She needs the opportunity to find solutions for herself.

It is tempting to intervene and tell her that she might fall and hurt herself; however, she will not learn from this. It is important to observe and see what she learns from the situation.

- If Sophie decides to stand on the bridge without testing it first then it makes sense to intervene, initially with questions, such as 'Do you think it will be safe if you walk on the bridge?' and 'How about we move the two tyres closer together to stop it wobbling?'. If she is still intent on walking on the bridge then you might have to inform her that it is not safe and she should not climb on it.

- If she realises that the task is not complete, then allow her to continue learning by making amendments to her structure. A confident child will have determination and perseverance.

- If she asks for help, then try encourage her as much to problem-solve for herself through discussion and questions before offering solutions.

Through this process Sophie will learn a great deal, develop and grow and you will learn a lot about her emerging physical, emotional and cognitive skills and abilities.

Chapter 10

ACTIVE LEARNING AND ENABLING ENVIRONMENTS

This chapter will look at how the environments children are exposed to will impact on their learning experience. This will include information for indoor space, outdoor space, providing opportunities to engage their learning, other spaces, and the people in their environment.

Enabling environments should be age specific, appealing to children's interests, making them feel happy, challenged, safe and secure and be a place where they can confidently play and learn. However, some of the best spaces will provide enriching and exciting spaces for children (and adults) of any age, either due to their nature or how they have been organised by professionals or a combination of both.

As children learn so much through exploring the environment and child-led activity, it is important that we create an environment that is interesting, exciting and poses challenges. With a well thought-out or chosen environment, children will be able to experiment, problem-solve, push themselves, use mathematical concepts, use their communication skills and be active with a minimum of input from adults.

Some questions to ask yourself when thinking about the environment include the following.

- Is it accessible for all?

- Do children feel cared for, safe and secure?

- Is the environment inviting to children?

- Will children experience many things without prompting from adults?

- Will children be stimulated by the environment?

- Will the environment challenge children to experiment, problem-solve and push themselves?

- Is the environment safe whilst still being challenging?

- Does the environment allow children to be flexible and is the environment itself flexible?

- Is the environment interesting for children?

Margaret McMillan, pioneer of the British nursery school, said, 'We are trying to create an environment where education will be almost inevitable.'[1] This is a simple explanation of an enabling environment. If it is interesting, exciting, enticing, encourages exploration, creativity and experimentation, it will enable learning.

When considering creating an enabling environment, you will need to take into account the emotional environment, the indoor environment and the outdoor environment.

EMOTIONAL ENVIRONMENT

The environment is not only the physical areas that children are exposed to but also the people who are in it: other children, parents/carers and staff. The emotional environment is affected by how parents/carers and staff interact, whether children feel safe, secure and cared for and if there is an underlying feeling of positivity or negativity in the space. In effect, relationships are what constitute the emotional environment, which includes the relationship between the parent/carer and staff, the relationship between staff and children, how people behave and speak to each other, how they are treated and how inclusive it is.

When children feel, safe, secure and happy in an environment that responds to their individual needs they are more likely to feel comfortable to try new things, push themselves and generally relax into enjoying their day. This will open them up to learning so many new things and allow them to be challenged physically, emotionally and cognitively.

---

1   Quoted in Hay, S. (2014) *Early Years Education and Care*. London: Routledge (p.106).

One of the best ways for children to learn is for them to feel comfortable to make mistakes and persevere until they get it right. Children will only be willing to do this if they are in a setting that has an emotional environment that encourages and supports all to explore and try new things.

It is therefore important for settings to have an ethos that supports positivity about failure, that nothing is wrong unless it will lead to someone getting hurt and trying something new is more important than sticking to your comfort zone. Much of this ethos will be discovered through adult role-modelling: we should allow ourselves to make mistakes, learn from them and try again, always be positive, allow children many opportunities for self-directed play and learning, respect each other and be inclusive.

INDOOR ENVIRONMENT

Indoor spaces need to be flexible to accommodate children's changing interests and needs, ensure there are spaces where children can be active and allow children to have an input into how the space is organised. If space is limited, consider activities such as dancing, active stories and yoga as they do not require a lot of space yet significantly raise the heart rate and allow children to learn at the same time.

The indoor environment will need to take children's changing interests and needs into account, and should be interesting and accessible to children.

OUTDOOR ENVIRONMENT

Children should be outdoors as much, if not more, as they are indoors and have a balance of self-directed and adult-let activity time. When children are outdoors they can play and explore without many of the restrictions that are so often placed on them. What they will encounter in nature is generally open-ended and will spark their imagination, encouraging them to discover and learn through their senses, leading to natural physical and cognitive development. Children can experience many things they are exposed to indoors, but often on a larger scale. This can be great for little hands that have not developed dexterity and fine-tuned their fine motor skills and for children who struggle to sit still and concentrate.

Creating an effective outdoor environment does not mean creating a pretty, tidy environment. Children love to explore wild spaces, enjoy messy play and be inspired by an array of what might appear to be junk. It is important not to place our aesthetic value on a space that has been created for children's exploration and enjoyment.

We also do not need to create different learning areas for subjects such as mathematics and literacy as children will constantly be learning if they are exposed to an enriching outdoor environment. As you will discover from other chapters, children will learn and develop so much if they are exposed to an enriching environment, allowed to explore, create and experiment and feel safe. When children play outside they learn about the effect they have on the world around them and how to be good to the environment. They will learn all kinds of mathematical concepts from outdoor activities, from playing with sticks, to water play, to building dens. They will develop their language and communication when role playing or problem-solving with their peers. Oh, and when they have finally built that bridge out of tyres and planks, they will feel so very good about themselves!

The provision of open-ended, non-prescriptive and adaptable resources will open up children's learning experience and encourage them to use their imagination, problem-solve and experiment.

Top Tip – The use of nature and inexpensive or recycled resources is all children really need when they are outdoors. See below for some ideas.

Resources

Ideas for natural and inexpensive resources to use in your outdoor area include:

- blackboard paint to use as permanent fixture
- chalk to create games on cemented surfaces
- strong cardboard packaging to create shelters
- pieces of fabric/old sheets to make tents and dens

- guttering to create a water play area
- tyres – these can be free from local garages
- planks, logs and pieces of wood
- signs
- boxes and crates to build with
- old CDs hanging at different levels
- old pots and pans strung on a strong line between trees with spoons to play them
- trellis for weaving thread or vines through
- shallow trays for water
- old wellingtons to plant in
- spare hosepipe wound along the fence with a funnel at each end to use as a telephone
- plastic drinks bottle filled with different substances and objects to hang or to create skittles
- the wonderful array of natural resources such as sand, water, mud, all types of earth, pebbles, stones and rocks
- feathers
- shells
- containers of various shapes and sizes
- painting equipment
- woodwork, gardening and DIY tools.

An enabling environment will allow a child to develop naturally through exploring, moving and experimenting. Allowing children independence, space and time to practice will enable them to excel.

Chapter 11

PHYSICAL ACTIVITY IDEAS

Children learn naturally when they are making use of the continuous provision and through child-directed play; however, we can enhance, challenge and help develop their learning through structured physical activities.

ENHANCING ACTIVITIES

Activities that take into account the points below will be more engaging and enjoyable for young children.

- Engage the imagination.
- Use active stories and active rhymes.
- Make use of animals in activities.
- Incorporate children's interests.
- Make use of music to encourage movement.
- Use action songs.

ELEMENTS OF PHYSICAL EDUCATION

Activities such as the following will help young children develop agility, balance, coordination and spatial awareness.

Gymnastics

- Learn Fundamental Movement Skills (FMS), mainly jumping, balancing and travelling
- Make shapes with their bodies
- Use large equipment
- Work in pairs
- Combine movements

Movement to Music and Dance

- Listen
- Make large and small movements
- Make fast and slow movements
- Combine movements
- Use these and other movements to learn body awareness
- Learn the 6 Dance Basics, using a variety of music including children's songs, classical, pop – see Chapter 11 for the dance basics

Games Competitive and Cooperative

- Team games, which can be competitive or cooperative (or a combination of both)
- Group games, which will be cooperative

Hand-Eye and Foot-Eye Coordination

- Ball skills – throwing, catching, kicking, striking, etc.
- Target games – aiming, estimating, predicting

HANDY BACK-UP RESOURCES

- Animal cards
- A music source
- Flash cards
- Bubbles
- Stories – improvise or use stories children are already familiar with
- Skills cards
- Fundamental Movement Skills

CROSS-BODY AND BILATERAL MOVEMENTS

Bilateral coordination is when we use both sides of our bodies independently from each other in the following ways:

- for the same action such as throwing a ball

- for different actions, such as throwing the ball with one hand and striking with a racket with the other hand

- for alternating the use of each side of the body, such as skipping, running, crawling, marching.

Cross-body movements are when you use one side of the body in the other side's space, relying on good bilateral coordination.

Efficient bilateral and cross-body coordination allows a child to use both hands and feet together for smooth movements and also supports the development of fine motor skills, reading and writing.

Top Tip – Rather than feeling that you should be investing in expensive resources, remember that you, physically, are an important resource for children's development. They will also gain a lot of learning and development from inexpensive open-ended recycled resources.

PHYSICAL EDUCATION LESSON OR STRUCTURED SESSIONS

Incorporating other areas of learning in a planned physical education lesson or structured session will support children's learning through fun experiences. You should include the following:

- counting and numbers to support mathematics

- using words and cooperative games to support literacy

- using interactive games to support social skills

- using animals, countries, different people, etc. to enhance activity and learn about the world around them

- ensuring all activities are inclusive and allow for achievement in order to develop confidence and self-esteem.

Top Tip – Do not spend too long on each activity during a physical education lesson as children may get bored and lose interest. In one lesson of approximately 45 minutes, children should take part in around five or six different activities, or variations of activities, including the warm up and cool down.

Top Tip – It can be useful to have a 'Focused' area of learning each week. Include this area of learning in your Physical Education Planning or Physical Development Planning for the week and plan a short focused activity around this area of leaning for each day.

PLANNING

Incorporate a physical activity section in the planning for all other areas or learning and subjects. This will allow you to include creative ways to help children learn through active and enjoyable activities.

MY ESSENTIAL RESOURCES

You do not need a huge amount of resources to create effective physical education lessons and adult-led activities. Giving children opportunities to play with no resources or equipment will spark their imagination and the possibilities are endless. However, simple resources used well can create exciting and imaginative activities that will enable children to develop and learn. Below are my essential resources that I would not leave the house without.

Mini Yo!

The Mini Yo! resource is a pack of 20 cards, each featuring a simplified yoga move. They are colourful, have instructions and are age-appropriate. The cards can be used by anyone who cares for young children, irrespective of their physical activity experience. The cards can be used for relaxing as well as more high-impact activities. I tend to use them for active stories the most by combining 3 or 4 to get my story started.[1]

---

1 Find out more about the Mini Yo! cards at www.binspireduk.co.uk/resources.

Alternatively, there are other similar yoga-based resources you can purchase and many videos online demonstrating yoga-based activities for children.

Mini Moves

The Mini Moves cards are a collection of movement skills children in the early years need to develop and animals to encourage them to move in different ways. I include the cards in well-known activities, such as obstacle courses, Traffic light game and Simon Says, but I also create many new activities using a selection of the cards.[2]

Alternatively, you can make your own cards using the Early Years Physical Skills in Chapter 2, along with your own images. You can also create animal and number cards with your own images. It is advisable to laminate these cards so you can use them over and over again.

Fantastic Elastic

Along with other props, such as balloons and streamers, Fantastic Elastic is a staple in my sessions. Instead of asking children to find a space and do various stretches and moves, holding the elastic in a circle helps them to focus and engage better and they find it fun.[3]

Music

Music is a very important aspect of child development, encouraging them to move in different ways, express themselves and be happy. Music can be used in many ways, singing, action songs, free movement, dancing and can be structured or child-directed. It can be used to occupy children during transitions from one activity to another. I also often play music at the beginning of a session, allowing children to move however they choose. This can help calm those with excess energy so that they are more able to focus on the more structured activities.

---

2 Find out more about the Mini Moves cards at www.binspireduk.co.uk/resources.

3 Find out more about Fantastic Elastic at www.binspireduk.co.uk/resources.

CHILD SPECIFIC

One of my favourites is Busy Feet CD by Health Matters Education, which has great action songs that are very energetic and catchy. The music CD comes as part of a pack of amazing resources, ideas and information about physical development and healthy eating.[4] Another favourite resource is Kimble's Music and Movement and Funky Feet Music – fantastic action songs CDs that not only encourage children to move but also underpin learning. They also provide workshops and activity sessions.[5]

CLASSICAL

Classical music is a great tool to help children understand different levels, tones, speed and develop their listening skills while moving.

POP

Children of all ages will respond to their current favourites; however, many older pop tunes will still get them moving, as long as they are appropriate for little ears. Vet the music first to avoid nasty surprises halfway through the song!

Rubber Spots

Rubber spots are an incredibly diverse and useful resource. Here are some examples of how they can be used:

- to help children to find a space by spreading them out in an area and asking children to stand on one (without moving it, which doesn't always work…)

- to encourage children to move around a full space, which will help children with spatial awareness. Unless an activity specifically needs children to move in a circle, always encourage them to use the whole space. Spreading the spots on the floor around a space and asking children to move amongst them (without standing on them) will help them to better understand the concept of using the whole space

---

4 www.healthmatterseducation.co.uk.

5 www.funkyfeetmusic.co.uk.

- for imaginative play. The spots can be rabbit holes when they pretend to be rabbits, hopping around the carrot field looking for carrots. The rabbit holes are where they need to hop back to when Mr Fox comes along! They can be superpower chargers for the Superheroes to the Rescue activity. They can also be magic rocks in the Magic Rocks and the Giant activity. They can also be lily pads to jump on in order to get across the river. Think of how many other things they can become
- to jump on, over, around
- for body-awareness activities, hiding the spot with different body parts
- for colour identification
- for counting, jumping from spot to spot while counting them
- in obstacle courses.

Beanbags

Beanbags are a great substitute for balls but can be used in so many different ways. For example, they can be used:

- for imaginative play. Beanbags can be small animals that need to be taken across a river or they can be food that the monkeys in Monkey Madness need to collect
- for target practice, as they can be easier to control than balls
- to balance on our bodies, which will help children to develop balance and control over themselves
- for body awareness activities, holding the beanbag with different body parts.

Markers

Markers can be used in the obvious way, marking where you would like children to move or not to move, but can also be used:

- as bowls to hold in little hands, using them to throw beanbags up in the air or to each other, instead of using their hands
- for target throwing (once children are confident in throwing into larger areas).

Cones

Cones can be used in a similar way to markers.

Balls

No selection of resources will be complete without a variety of balls of different sizes, weight and materials. Not only is it important to teach children to throw, catch, kick and hit or strike them, but they are useful for many games and most children will need little encouragement to move and play if they are given a ball. Having a selection of sizes will make your activities inclusive for all children, irrespective of ability.

Bats

Simple plastic bats are not only useful for hitting but can be used for carrying and dribbling balls on the ground.

ACTIVITIES A–Z

Many physical activities that we do with children on a daily basis support learning and development in many ways that are not obvious. This chapter contains activity ideas that can be used individually or in a physical education lesson. Some of these activities have been around for a long time (because they work!) and others are new ideas.

With the use of differentiation, each activity can be simplified or made more challenging depending on the age and development level of the children you care for. The same process can be used for children with special educational needs, as they are all individuals with different levels of ability.

ACTIVE ALPHABET

In a large space work your way through the different letters of the alphabet by acting out the following moves or make up your own.

Equipment

Music; Balls; Mini Yo! cards (or your imagination)

* **A** – Arm movements
* **B** – Balancing

* **C** – Cat (Mini Yo!)
* **D** – Dance
* **E** – Elephant (Mini Yo! or pretend to be an elephant)
* **F** – Frog (Mini Yo! or pretend to be a frog)
* **G** – Gorilla (Mini Yo! or pretend to be a gorilla)
* **H** – Hopping
* **I** – In and Out (weave in and out each other or a piece of apparatus)
* **J** – Jumping
* **K** – Kicking (a ball)
* **L** – Leaping, Lion Jumping
* **M** – Mountain (Mini Yo!) or March
* **N** – Nod your head
* **O** – Owl (fly around)
* **P** – Pointing (point to the left, point to the right, point up, point down, etc.)
* **Q** – Quick Movements
* **R** – Rock (Mini Yo!)
* **S** – Skipping
* **T** – Tiptoe
* **U** – Up (let's start as small seeds and grow up into tall flowers)
* **V** – Vegetables (stand tall and thin like a carrot, become round and big like a potato, etc.)
* **W** – Warrior
* **X** – X looks like a cross! Cross over your feet, can you balance?
* **Y** – Yoga (Mini Yo!)
* **Z** – Zebra

We just went from letter to letter and had fun with it!

Benefits

Supports gross motor development, spatial awareness, language, communication and thinking skills.

Areas of Learning this Activity Covers
  * Expressive arts, design and creative development
  * Knowledge of and understanding the world
  * Language, literacy and communication
  * Personal, social and emotional development

ACTIVE CUBE

Equipment

Active cube with transparent wallets; paper (sized to fit into the wallets); mark makers such as crayons, pencils; pictures of moves; images of skills, numbers, fruit, animals, etc.

Initially place image cards in each wallet. Children to take turns to roll or throw the cube. Children act out image on face-up pocket of cube.

Children's Imagination Ideas
  1. Using topics and interests, give each child a piece of paper that fits into the cube pockets and mark makers.
  2. Show children pictures of the dragon running very fast, the fairy hopping on her tiptoes, the pirate bending down to pick up the treasure, etc.
  3. Show them the word that goes with the picture, e.g. run, hop, bend.
  4. Can you write the word on the paper? Support them to write the word.
  5. Once children have completed the words place them in the wallets of the active cube.
  6. Throw the cube and when it lands, get all to copy the move in face-up pocket.
  7. Now we are going to run fast like a dragon, etc.

Benefits

Supports the development of gross and fine motor skills, spatial awareness, and balance; helps children to use their imagination.

Areas of Learning this Activity Covers
  * Expressive arts, design and creative development

* Knowledge of and understanding the world
* Language, literacy and communication
* Mathematics and numeracy
* Personal, Social and Emotional Development
* Social, Moral, Spiritual and Cultural Development

ACTIVE STORIES

To create an active story decide on the skills/moves/subject matter (e.g., animal in the jungle, going to the supermarket, space travel). Some points to bear in mind include the following:

- The story can be very simple as it is all about the movement; however do try to create a journey of some sort.
- Older children can help with the story, such as deciding on the animal, what they would like to purchase at the supermarket, etc.
- Physical skills and movement can be incorporated into any story.
- Active stories can be created from any story children are aware of and love.

Creating a Story

Active stories can be based on just about anything, such as:

- everyday activities – driving the car, the car wash, shopping
- adventures – holiday in the jungle, journey to the bottom of the sea
- emotions
- superheroes
- going to the farm.

The possibilities for actions are endless. I've given some examples below.

Driving the car, children can:

- steer
- wipe the windscreen with the wipers
- bounce over humps on the road
- drive on a nice smooth road
- drive on a bumpy dirt road

- screech to a stop
- turn left, turn right
- go round a roundabout
- stop, wait and go at the traffic light
- turn on the headlights
- use the indicators.

On a farm, children can:

- gallop like a horse
- drive a tractor
- roll around like a pig in the mud
- be chased by a bull
- try to catch a chicken
- collect eggs
- jump off hay bales
- spring like lambs in a field.

In the jungle, children can:

- roar like a bear
- bound like a cheeky monkey
- climb a tree like a sloth
- fly like a butterfly
- slither like a snake
- bend or crouch under tree branches
- jump over streams and logs
- be chased by a tiger
- swat mosquitoes
- tiptoe past the sleeping elephant.

FUN IN THE FOREST

Using movement skills create a forest adventure encouraging children to move in different ways. The forest adventure can be repeated on a regular basis with different skills (e.g. bend, gallop, leap, wiggle). Explain to the children that:

* It's a beautiful day and we are going on an adventure through the forest.
* If we come across any streams of water we need to leap over them.
* If we find any hills we should gallop up and then down them.
* If we find ourselves stuck in brambles we will have to wiggle our way out.
* If we need to go past any trees we need to bend under the branches.

Move through the forest and regularly find yourselves at a tree, stream, hill or brambles, see if the children can remember what to do when they reach them.

Help children to develop their imagination and independence by asking them to create their own stories, supported by the following questions.

* What do you want your story to be about (interests)?
* What are you going to be in your story?
* Where will you be?
* Where will you go?
* What are you going to do/look for?
* Why?
* Can you draw a picture of your story? If they are able to, ask them to write their story down.

Repeat active stories on a regular basis with small changes. For example, instead of gallop, incorporate spin, where a child needs to spin every time the wind blows through the forest, Be creative and add props to the stories.

Benefits
Supports gross motor development, independence, imagination, creative thinking and fine motor skills (drawing and writing) as well as other areas of learning.

Areas of Learning this Activity Covers
* Expressive arts, design and creative development
* Knowledge of and understanding the world

* Language, literacy and communication
* Mathematics and numeracy
* Personal, social and emotional development
* Social, Moral, Spiritual and Cultural Development

AIM AND SCORE

Equipment

Beanbags; hula hoops

Instructions

Divide children into small groups and line up behind the start line.

Place hula hoops a short distance away from the start line in front of each group.

Place the same number of beanbags as children on the start line.

On the 'go' command, the children at the front of each line should try throwing a beanbag into their hula hoop.

That child moves to the back of the line and the next child steps forward to the start line, picks up a beanbag and tries to throw it in the hula hoop.

Each child in the groups takes a turn to try throwing a beanbag into their hula hoop.

Each team score a point for each beanbag that was thrown correctly into their hula hoop.

Think about how children can keep record of their scores?

Next place three hula hoops in front of each line – near, middle distance and far.

Each child takes a turn to try throw in one of their hula hoops.

The teams score:

- One point for each beanbag thrown in the near hula hoop
- Two points for each beanbag thrown into the middle distance hula hoop
- Three points for each beanbag thrown into the far hula hoop.

This does not necessarily have to be a competition between the groups; it can help them to learn cooperative play, score taking and numbers.

Benefits

This helps to develop children's skills such as throwing and aiming. It also supports other areas of learning such as mathematics and social skills, as well as hand-eye coordination, spatial awareness, taking turns and problem-solving.

Areas of Learning this Activity Covers

* Mathematics and numeracy
* Personal, Social and Emotional Development
* Social, Moral, Spiritual and Cultural Development

ANIMAL OBSTACLE COURSES

Set up courses that will encourage children to move their bodies in different ways, throw, catch, kick, climb over objects, crawl through tunnels or slither under equipment.

Encourage different movements and skills such as running in and out of cones, jumping from spot to spot, carrying beanbags on different body parts, and skipping from place to place.

Challenge children to travel in different ways, e.g. walk, run, hop, skip, jump, walk backwards.

Use soft play equipment for rolling, sliding and crawling.

Place the picture of an animal next to the different sections of the course to encourage children to move in that way. The imaginative aspect will make the activity interesting and exciting for children.

Encourage children to create their own courses and share with other children.

Include climbing, swinging and hanging activities to help develop upper body strength.

Sneak in a fine motor skill such as digging in the sand pit, using tongs to place pom-poms into a container or threading beads. This is great for children who find it hard to sit still to do fine motor activities.

When children are confident with other games/activities combine them to make obstacle courses, e.g. Beanbag Relay Race (throw a beanbag into a container), Jumping and Hopping activity, Balancing and Tightrope.

Benefits

These develop gross motor skills (and fine motor skills), balance, coordination, spatial awareness, agility, pathways and hand-eye coordination.

Areas of Learning this Activity Covers

* Expressive arts, design and creative development
* Knowledge of and understanding the world

BALL STOP

Give each child a ball.

Instruct them to roll the ball and chase it.

Call out a body part and the child will need to stop the ball with that part of the body.

or

Divide children into pairs.

One child rolls a ball and the other child chases it.

Call out a body part and the child who is chasing the ball will need to stop the ball with that part of the body.

Benefits

This develops gross motor skills, coordination, spatial awareness and hand-eye coordination.

Areas of Learning this Activity Covers

* Expressive arts, design and creative development
* Knowledge of and understanding the World
* Language, literacy and communication
* Mathematics and numeracy
* Personal, Social and Emotional Development.

BEANBAG RELAY RACES

In a large area scatter the same number of beanbags as the number of children.

Divide children into small groups.

Give each group a container.

Explain that each group needs to stand in a straight line behind the start line.

On 'go' the children at the front of each line run and collect a beanbag.

They run back to their group and place the beanbag in their container.

Once they have placed their beanbag in their container the next child goes.

Once all beanbags have been collected the game ends.

Once children have mastered this, allocate a different skill to each person, e.g. first person in each row skips, second person in each row hops.

If there are any children with special educational needs in the group, allocate the skills that they can attain to the line that they are in.

Next, ask children who are waiting their turn to do the allocated skill on the spot, hence they will be doing the same skill on the spot that the child who is collecting the beanbag at the time will be doing.

The aim of the game is not to race against each other, it is to see how fast they can all collect the beanbags.

Place smaller objects on the floor instead of beanbags to help develop fine motor skills.

Benefits

Good for developing gross motor, fine motor, spatial awareness skills, agility, getting children active and teaching them about taking turns and working together.

Areas of Learning this Activity Covers

  * Personal, Social and Emotional Development
  * Mathematics and numeracy
  * Social, Moral, Spiritual and Cultural Development

BIGGER! 'HEAD, SHOULDERS, KNEES AND TOES'

Once children have learnt and can do 'Heads, shoulders, knees and toes' standing try it sitting with feet in the air.

Sit on the floor, pull stomachs in tight and lift feet off the floor.

Touch each body part that corresponds with the rhyme keeping only your bottom in contact with the floor.

Now try doing it backwards!

Benefits

Good for developing core strength, balance, body awareness, listening skills and communication.

Areas of Learning this Activity Covers

* Expressive arts, design and creative development
* Knowledge of and understanding the World
* Language, literacy and communication

BIG NURSERY RHYMES

Choose a nursery rhyme.

Create big, energetic moves to the rhyme.

The more you move up and down the more energy you will use.

Older children can help create the moves.

Benefits

Can support skills, other areas of learning, topics, imagination, spatial awareness and children reluctant to do physical activities.

Areas of Learning this Activity Covers

* Expressive arts, design and creative development
* Language, literacy and communication
* Personal, Social and Emotional Development
* Social, Moral, Spiritual and Cultural Development

CATS AND RABBITS

Split children into two groups. One group to be cats and the other to be rabbits.

On your command, the cats move around on all fours chasing the rabbits who hop around the area.

On your command, the rabbits become cats and the cats become rabbits.

These can be substituted for different animals and ways to move around.

Benefits

This develops gross motor skills, fine motor skills, balance, coordination and spatial awareness.

Areas of Learning this Activity Covers

* Expressive arts, design and creative development
* Language, literacy and communication
* Knowledge of and understanding the world
* Social, Moral, Spiritual and Cultural Development

CONE CATCHES

Equipment

A3 card for each child; markers; scissors; sticking tape; soft balls

Instructions

Give each child a piece of card and a pair of scissors.

Draw lines from two corners to opposite centre to create a triangle shape that will allow it to be made into a cone.

Help them to cut the card on the lines.

Children can then decorate their card with the markers.

Ask them to write their name on their card.

Stick two of the edges together to create a cone.

Child holds the cone with both hands.

Place a small light ball in the cone (such as balls from ball pools).

Show the children how you throw the ball up with the cone and then try to catch it in the cone.

Once children start to confidently throw and catch the ball by themselves, pair them up.

One child should put their cone down and the other puts their ball down.

The child with the ball throws the ball while the other tries to catch it in the cone.

Do this until the child catches the ball.

They then swap throwing and catching.

If any child finds this difficult, pair them up with an adult who can help direct the throws and catches.

Benefits

Supports gross and fine motor skills, throwing and catching, hand-eye coordination, balance, spatial awareness and problem-solving skills. This will help children develop catching skills, making it easier for them to catch a large ball with their hands.

Areas of Learning this Activity Covers

* Expressive arts, design and creative development
* Knowledge of and understanding the world
* Language, literacy and communication
* Mathematics and numeracy
* Personal, social and emotional development
* Social, Moral, Spiritual and Cultural Development

COLOURS

Start with traffic light colours: Red means stop, Green means go, Amber means jump up and down on the spot.

When 'Red' prompt is called, ensure that the children stand still for at least 10 seconds (this helps develops balance).

Add additional colours to link with skills, e.g. Purple can mean hop, Blue can mean run.

To develop children's balance further, instruct them to stand on one foot when 'Red' prompt is called out.

Children can select their own colours and moves.

Benefits

Supports gross motor skills, other areas of learning, topics, imagination, spatial awareness, balance, and encourages children reluctant to do physical activities. When children stand still for an extended period of time it helps with balance and to build muscle strength.

Areas of Learning this Activity Covers

* Expressive arts, design and creative development
* Knowledge of and understanding the world
* Language, literacy and communication
* Social, Moral, Spiritual and Cultural Development

FANTASTIC ELASTIC

Equipment

4-metre elastic circle

Activity 1

Maximum 10 children per group.

1. All children stand in a circle and hold onto the fantastic elastic with both hands
2. Take one step backwards
3. Take one step forwards
4. Move to the left
5. Move to the right
6. Stretch up with the elastic high in the air
7. Crouch down and put the elastic on the floor
8. Stand up
9. Climb over the elastic into the elastic circle
10. Climb under the elastic outside the elastic circle

11. Sit down and hook the elastic with your feet (if possible don't place hands and knees on the floor to support sitting down)

12. Raise your feet into the air

13. Stand up (if possible don't place hands and knees on the floor to support standing up)

14. Hook the elastic in the crook of your arms, think of other body parts you can hold the elastic with

15. Create shapes with the elastic, such as square, triangle, rectangle, etc.

16. What else can you think of doing?

Activity 2

Two children stand facing each other approximately two metres apart, holding the elastic with both hands. The elastic should be tight but not too tight (children should still find it easy to move the elastic).

The rest of the group stand in a line facing the middle of the elastic.

Some suggested ways for children to move from one side of the elastic to the other:

- Over the elastic
- Under the elastic
- Through the elastic
- Around the elastic
- Outside the elastic
- Inside the elastic
- Diagonally over the elastic
- Diagonally under the elastic
- Jump above the elastic
- Squat below the elastic
- Stand in the middle of the elastic and turn left then turn right
- Pair up the children and ask them to help each other over, under or through the elastic
- Ask each pair to hold hands and move over, under or through the elastic
- Can you think of any other ways to move from one side to the other?

Benefits

Fantastic Elastic can support gross motor skills development, fine motor skills, balance, coordination, spatial awareness, other areas of learning, such as mathematics, language and communication, as well as help children to focus and develop their listening skills.

Areas of Learning this Activity Covers

* Language, literacy and communication
* Mathematics and numeracy
* Personal, Social and Emotional Development

FLYING CREATURES

In a large space mark out a line that children should stand behind and then further parallel lines at one metre intervals.

Split children into equal numbered groups (approximately 10 children).

Provide children with a variety of non-breakable resources and toys.

Each child from the first group selects one object, which will be their creature, and stands behind the line.

On the count of three, children should throw their 'creatures' as far as they can.

Make a note of how far each 'creature' was thrown.

Repeat with the other groups, using the same 'creatures'.

Have a discussion about:

- What creature was thrown the furthest on each throw?
- What creature was thrown the furthest most times?
- What creature travelled the least?
- What creature is the heaviest?
- How far did the heaviest creature travel?
- What creature was the lightest, biggest, smallest, strangest shape, etc.?
- How far did each of the creatures travel?
- Compare the distance that each child threw, etc.

Benefits

Gross motor skills (throwing), mathematics, measuring, sorting, comparing and contrasting, turn taking.

Areas of Learning this Activity Covers

 * Mathematics and numeracy
 * Language, literacy and communication
 * Expressive arts, design and creative development
 * Knowledge of and understanding the world

LETTER RUN AROUND

Equipment

Cards with graphemes or letters (depending on children's age and ability)

Instructions

Outside or in a large indoor area give each child one card (two children should have the same letter or grapheme).

Children sit in a circle.

Call out one of the letters or graphemes.

The children who have that letter or grapheme need to run around the circle and sit back down where they started.

Once children have all had a turn, include skills, such as hop around the circle, rather than run.

If children are older, they can have a turn to call out a letter other than their own.

Benefits

Supports the development of gross and fine motor skills, letter or sound recognition, thinking skills, memory skills, spatial awareness and cooperative play.

Areas of Learning this Activity Covers

 * Knowledge of and understanding the world
 * Language, literacy and communication
 * Personal, Social and Emotional Development

MAGIC ROCKS AND THE GIANT (HIDE THE SPOT!)

Equipment

One spot per child and adult

Instructions

Spread spots out so that there is enough space for all to move around between them.

First, instruct children to stand on a spot and instruct them to:

- Hide the spot with their feet – stand on the spot
- Hide the spot with their knees – kneel on the spot
- Hide the spot with their bottom – sit on the spot
- Hide the spot with their hands – put their hands on the spot
- Hide the spot with their stomach – lie stomach down on the spot
- Hide the spot with their back – lie backwards on the spot
- Hide the spot with their chin – put their chin on the spot
- What else can they hide the spot with?

Next tell children that the spots are magic rocks on an island. Explain that the spots are magic rocks that need to be protected from the 'giant' (the adult).

Children should move in amongst the 'rocks' in different ways (physical skills).

When the adult shouts out a body part the children need to find a 'rock' and hide it with that body part, while the 'giant' tries to find a magic rock.

Benefits

This can support spatial awareness (body awareness), gross motor development and imagination.

Areas of Learning this Activity Covers

- * Expressive arts, design and creative development
- * Language, literacy and communication
- * Social, Moral, Spiritual and Cultural Development

MINI YO! (OR OTHER YOGA-BASED RESOURCES)[6]

Warm Ups and Relaxation

Mini Yo! moves can be used individually to warm up and stretch before or after any high impact physical session activity. They can also be used to help children to relax, and use their imagination.

Medium Impact Activities

Most moves executed on their own will not raise the heart rate a great deal; however, they will support the development of the child's physical ability and strength.

Active Stories

Demonstrate a selection of moves for children to do. Once children feel comfortable performing the moves individually, create an active story with a selection of moves. Tell a story using three or four different moves. Encourage children to use the whole area as you go on your journey. If a mix of standing, sitting and lying down positions is used, you are more likely to raise their heart rate.

Alphabet

Using the 'Alphabet' card, demonstrate moves that start with the letters of the alphabet.

Help children to spell their names using their bodies.

Ask if children can write their names?

Now ask if they can spell their names with the Mini Yo! moves? For example, S for Snake, A for Aeroplane and M for Mountain spells SAM.

Suggest that if there is no move for a letter in a child's name, they create a move or look at the alphabet card to see what they should do.

Benefits

Supports gross motor development, balance, independence, imagination and fine motor skills.

Areas of Learning this Activity Covers

* Expressive arts, design and creative development
* Knowledge of and understanding the world

---

6   See www.binspired.co.uk/resources.

* Language, literacy and communication
* Personal, Social and Emotional Development
* Social, Moral, Spiritual and Cultural Development

MONKEY MADNESS

Equipment

3 balls or 2 beanbags and 1 ball per team to use as 'fruit'.

Instructions

Divide children into groups of up to six.

Each team should stand in a line shoulder to shoulder.

Say, 'Let's pretend we are all monkeys collecting lots of fruit'.

1. First, children can pass the ball or beanbags to each other in any way that they like

2. To progress, the teams first pass each ball or beanbag with their right hand only (make a mark or place stickers on the right hand if they are still learning left from right)

3. The child at the end of the line should drop the 'fruit' and shout 'Monkey Go!' for the first child to pass the next 'piece of fruit'

4. Repeat step 2 but with left hands

5. Repeat step 3

6. Then bounce the ball sideways to each other, children can catch with one or two hands

7. If a 'piece of fruit' is dropped it must be returned to the beginning of the line and that task needs to be started again

8. When they have finished passing all the 'fruit', the whole group should pretend to be monkeys and should all make monkey noises!

Benefits

Can support coordination, basic skills, social skills, cooperative play, listening skills, spatial awareness and taking turns.

Areas of Learning this Activity Covers
* * Expressive arts, design and creative development
* * Knowledge of and understanding the world
* * Language, literacy and communication
* * Personal, Social and Emotional Development
* * Social, Moral, Spiritual and Cultural Development

MOVEMENT TO MUSIC AND DANCES

There are different ways to use music to support children's physical development and to encourage them to move, including;

* Free movement to music
* Move faster and slower to tempo
* Move higher and lower to levels of music
* Move with different weight, e.g. stomp and tip toe to music
* Body-part movement – moving individual body parts whilst also moving to the music
* Move props to music – give children a selection of resources that they can move to the music while they are moving.
* Create stories to music
* Use the Dance Basics to create dances.

The Six Dance Basics

* Jump – on the spot or from place to place
* Gesture – forwards, backwards, up/down, side to side.
* Stillness – standing, crouching, bending, sitting, lying, etc.
* Turn – in big circles, spinning, one way, both ways, etc.
* Travel – fast, slow, backwards, forwards, move whilst going up and down, etc.
* Fall – fast, slow, fall to hands, lower to bottoms, etc.

Benefits

Children need to develop good spatial awareness and coordination to perform dances and to move to music in groups. Can support many basic skills, balance and brain development (crossing the midline).

MUSICAL STATUE CHAMPIONS

Play music children enjoy.

Children move in any manner they want around the space, avoiding each other.

Stop the music – children should stop and keep still (the longer they remain still the better, as young children will need to learn how to manage their bodies to keep still).

Children who can keep still will become Statue Champions.

VARIATIONS

- Children move around the space in the manner of the various skills of the week.
- Children should not smile when they stop (this can be fun as they will then want to smile).
- When the music stops children need to stop and stay still on one foot, one foot and one hand, on their bottoms and nothing else, etc.

In pairs

Place children into pairs and allocate statue to one child and champion to other child. The 'statue' stays still while the music plays and the 'champion' moves around the space while the music plays.

When the music stops the 'champion' must find their statue and touch them.

Once they have touched their 'statue' they become the 'statue' and their friend becomes the 'champion' (changing roles).

Once the music starts the new 'statues' stay still and the new 'champions' move around the space.

Repeat.

Benefits

Supports the development of gross motor skills, balance, coordination, spatial awareness, body control, imagination, communication, concentration and listening skills.

Areas of Learning this Activity Covers

- * Expressive arts, design and creative development
- * Personal, Social and Emotional Development

FEATHER DANCE

Ask children to pretend they have a bag full of transparent feathers. Throw them as high in the air as they can.

Pretend the feathers are floating around the room, we can't see them but we can feel them.

Play gentle music and ask them to move parts of their body to music, pretending that transparent feather are landing on them.

Demonstrate how you move a part of your body when a feather lands on it.

Explore different ways that the body parts can move.

Eventually challenge them to refine their movements by challenging them to keep their whole body still while only moving the selected body part.

Next ask them to move two body parts at the same time.

Once they are able to do this, ask the children to move to the music and when you shout a body part they move to the music and move that body part at the same time.

Once all the transparent feathers have fallen to the ground ask them to pretend they have brooms in their hands.

Sweep the transparent feathers away in time to the music.

This can be repeated with faster or slower music.

Benefits
Supports the development of gross motor skills, balance, coordination, spatial awareness, body awareness, imagination, communication and listening skills.

Areas of Learning this Activity Covers
* Expressive arts, design and creative development
* Language, literacy and communication

LISTEN AND MOVE

Use music that changes tempo, speed, levels, etc. Classical music is always good for this.

Children initially move around the space in any manner they please, avoiding each other and other objects.

Next, explain that the music goes faster and slower and we need to change our speed when the music does. This will help them to learn the rhythm of the music.

Once they are confidently moving to the music's rhythm, allocate different movements to different instruments, e.g. moving on tiptoes when the music has a light airy feel and stomping around when the music is full of bass or drums.

Benefits

Supports the development of gross motor skills, balance, coordination, spatial awareness, body awareness, imagination, learning patterns and listening skills.

Areas of Learning this Activity Covers

* Expressive arts, design and creative development
* Mathematics and numeracy
* Language, literacy and communication

RIBBON DANCE

You can use ribbons or resources you already have but if children make their own this will support both gross and fine motor development.

To make your own use:

- curling ribbon
- large elastic bands
- scissors.

Cut long strips of curling ribbon (various colours).

Fold 3 or 4 ribbons in half and attach to an elastic band (make sure the elastic band fits loosely on child's wrist).

Encourage children to move around the space while moving their arms, which will make the ribbon move.

Encourage them to move their arms:

- forwards and backwards
- in and out

- side to side
- around in circles backwards
- around in circles forwards.

Benefits

This supports development of shoulder muscles, fine and gross motor skills, coordination and spatial/body awareness.

Areas of Learning this Activity Covers

* Expressive arts, design and creative development
* Language, literacy and communication

DANCING STORIES

Using current topics, create simple movements to the music that can become a very simple story to music.

Examples

DRAGONS AND FAIRIES

Move to different parts of the music like a dragon, a fairy, trees, sky, etc.

A fairy is flying through the forest and sees a dragon breathing fire. She watches from behind a tree. The dragon sees her and she flies into the sky. The dragon follows her as he is curious to find out what she is. They fly high into the sky and start to play flying in circles, up and down, etc.

UNDER THE SEA

Ask children to think of what they will find under the sea.

We're all little fish swimming in the sea. We come to some seaweed which is swishing about in different ways with the movement of the water. We then come to a shark that is swimming very menacingly, we swim away very quickly and find a starfish moving slowly on the sea bed, etc.

Benefits

Can support skills, balance, spatial awareness, coordination and gross motor development, body awareness, communication, language and listening skills.

Areas of Learning this Activity Covers
  * Expressive arts, design and creative development
  * Knowledge of and understanding the world
  * Language, literacy and communication
  * Personal, social and emotional development
  * Social, Moral, Spiritual and Cultural Development

MUSICAL GROUPS

Outdoors or in a large indoor area, draw or mark out large shapes on the ground.

Play music and instruct children to move around the area in different ways (mimicing animals, moving in a specific way, etc.).

When the music stops children have to move into a shape.

Ask children a question such as:

  * How many people are in your group? How do you know?
  * Do you have more or less children in your group than the group next to you?
  * How many hands are in your group?
  * How many girls, how many boys are in your group?
  * How can we make each group the same? Do some of you need to move to a different group? How can we do this?

After each question, play the music again and children need to move in a different way.

Stop music and children should move to a shape, once again.

Ask another question.

Repeat.

Benefits
Gross motor development, spatial awareness, social skills, mathematics, cooperation, problem-solving.

Areas of Learning this Activity Covers
  * Expressive arts, design and creative development
  * Knowledge and understanding of the world

* Language, literacy and communication
* Personal, social and emotional development
* Mathematics and numeracy
* Social, Moral, Spiritual and Cultural Development

NUMBER CIRCLE

In a large room or outdoor space, place cards such as Mini Moves cards from numbers 1–10 (with animals on one side of the card and numbers on the other side) in a circle around the edge with numbers facing up.

All children should stay inside the number cards.

Play some music children enjoy moving to.

Call out a number.

Children should run to that number.

Children identify the animal on the back and move like that animal to the music.

Repeat.

When children find this easy, ask questions where one of the number cards will be the answer. Get children to move to the card that they think is the answer. This might be too challenging for three-year-olds!

Question ideas:

- What number comes between 6 and 8?
- What numbers are smaller than 3
- What is 2 + 2?
- How many fingers do you have?
- How many girls are there?

Ask children to explain why they chose a particular number as their answer.

Benefits

These activities support the development of gross motor skills, spatial awareness, mathematics, problem-solving and social skills.

Areas of Learning this Activity Covers
- *   Mathematics and numeracy
- *   Personal, Social and Emotional Development
- *   Language, literacy and communication

NUMBER HUNTS

Use cards with numbers on one side and animals on the other side (e.g. Mini Moves cards).

Hide one number per child in the outdoor or large indoor area (number 1–10, more than one of each number if more than 10 children).

Explain to children that the numbers are all over the area, including climbing equipment, bushes, etc.

Instruct children to search for a number and return, acting out the animal on the back of the card when they find one.

When all children have returned ask them to arrange themselves in a line.

Ask them questions that are appropriate for their age, such as:
- Can you line up with the smallest number one end and the largest number at the other end?
- Put your hand up if your number is lower than six.
- Which number goes before five?
- Which number goes after eight?
- Which number is the smallest number?
- Which number is the largest number?
- Which number has two round circles/ which number has a straight line and a circle, etc.?

Benefits

These activities support the development of gross motor skills, fine motor skills, mathematics, problem-solving and social skills.

Areas of Learning this Activity Covers
- *   Mathematics and numeracy
- *   Personal, Social and Emotional Development

NUMBER RUN

This activity works best outdoors or in a large indoor space.

Place a ball next to you.

Allocate a number to each child (if possible try keep the group small – up to 10 children).

Children need to run around the space or move in different ways (physical skills) and when you call out their number, they need to run towards the ball and kick it.

Provide a large target for them to attempt to kick the ball towards.

Instruct children to stop and then attempt to kick the ball towards the target.

When each child has had a turn get them to travel in different ways on your command, e.g. hop, jump, crawl.

Progression

After each child has practiced kicking the ball from standing and all or most are confident doing it, encourage them to kick from running (without stopping).

Benefits

Spatial awareness, balance, coordination, mathematics, kicking, basic skills, taking turns.

Areas of Learning this Activity Covers

* Mathematics and numeracy

PAPER FORTUNE TELLER

Start by making a square out of an A4 piece of paper by folding one corner of the paper over to the adjacent side.

Cut off the small rectangle, forming the square, which is already folded into a triangle.

Fold the two opposite ends of the triangle together, forming a smaller triangle.

Unfold all the folds.

Fold one corner into the central point. Repeat with the opposite corner and then the other two corners.

Flip the paper over.

Fold a corner over to the centre. Repeat with the opposite corner and then the other two corners. You will end up with a small square.

Fold the square in half, then unfold and fold in half the other way.

Unfold and pull the four ends together, making a diamond-like shape. Pick up each of the four square flaps, and put your fingers inside. You will be able to move the four parts around.

Write any four colours on the four flaps.

Flip it over, and write eight numbers on the triangular flaps.

Write eight active fortunes inside the flaps underneath the numbers.

Examples of fortunes:
- Touch your toes five times
- Balance on one foot
- Jump seven times
- Hop two times on each foot
- Hop like a bunny rabbit five times
- Leap like a leopard four times
- Stomp like an elephant six times.

First, demonstrate how it works, then pair up children so they can take turns with one child moving the fortune teller and the other selecting the colours and numbers and then performing the fortune.

Differentiation

This will be too complicated for young children to make, so you could make one and all children could follow your instructions (or one child is the leader and moves the fortune teller and the rest of the group act out the fortune). If possible, make a few and the children can decorate them. If children are writing on the fortune teller, they may need help as the space is small.

Benefits

Supports fine and gross motor development, social skills, mathematics and literacy.

Areas of Learning this Activity Covers

* Expressive arts, design and creative development
* Language, literacy and communication
* Mathematics and numeracy
* Personal, Social and Emotional Development

PROPS

Equipment

Balloon; tinfoil; playdough or anything malleable

Instructions

In this activity, the children mimic what you do with your prop.

Using the balloon:

1. Stretch it from top to bottom – children to stretch up high on tiptoes.

2. Stretch it from side to side – children to stretch their arms and legs out to the side.

3. Scrunch into a ball – all to curl into a ball.

4. Blow the balloon up – all to become as round and big as they can.

5. Let the balloon go – all to run around like a wriggling balloon and then fall on the ground.

6. Repeat all the moves.

7. What else can you use?

Benefits

Can support gross motor skills, other areas of learning, topics, imagination, spatial awareness, concentration, listening skills.

Areas of Learning this Activity Covers

* Expressive arts, design and creative development
* Language, literacy and communication
* Personal, Social and Emotional Development

SHADOWS

Instruct children to be your shadow, copying every move you make. Move in different ways, fast and slowly.

Next place children in pairs. One child should copy the other child's movements.

At first, let children move in any way they choose.

Swap places.

Next, instruct the lead child to move in a certain way (physical skills, animals, etc.). They should move around the area using the specified movement and the other child should continue to shadow them.

Swap places.

This could lead into a follow-the-leader game where children are split into groups of 8–10 children and the group follows the leader's moves.

Benefits

Develops gross motor skills, spatial awareness, pathways, comm-unication, concentration and teaches children to mimic others.

Areas of Learning this Activity Covers

* Expressive arts, design and creative development
* Language, literacy and communication
* Personal, Social and Emotional Development
* Social, Moral, Spiritual and Cultural Development

SLOW MO

Slowing down activities and movement.
Try the following slowly:

- Walking up and down stairs
- Riding a pretend bicycle lying on your back
- Running a race (winner is last person to cross the line)
- Pretending to be animals racing each other (winner is last person to cross the line)
- Shooting a basketball
- Ballet dancing

- Karate kicks
- Boxing
- Skipping rope
- Dancing.

Benefits

Moving slowly can support skills, balance. Slowing down motions require more muscle control and a longer muscle contraction. Many activities performed slowly can be more challenging as you will require better balance and control. Children will also need to concentrate more on what they are doing.

Areas of Learning this Activity Covers

* Expressive arts, design and creative development
* Knowledge and understanding the world
* Language, literacy and communication

SUPERHEROES TO THE RESCUE

Equipment

One spot per child

Instructions

Place spots in a corner of a large area, spaced out so children can stand on them.

Tell children you are all going to be superheroes and are going to save people and things.

Next tell them what superhero you are and ask them what superhero they would like to be, giving suggestions such as Spider-man, Superman, Ben 10, Batgirl, Batman, Power Rangers, etc.

The spots are the superheroes' superpower chargers.

All to stand on a spot and adopt their superhero pose.

Say, 'Superheroes, there is a building on fire. Shall we go save the people and put the fire out?'

Once they have all agreed, put an arm in the air like a flying superhero and tell them to adopt the flying pose.

Tell them to follow you and all run around until you decide you have reached the building.

Climb the building, pick up the people, jump out, all to take 3 deep breaths and blow out the fire with their super breath.

'Well done, superheroes! You've saved the people.'

You now need to go back to recharge your superpowers.

Raise one arm in the air and all fly back, ensure to tell them to follow you, and run back.

Other ideas – Stop two trains from crashing, pull a car out of the river, save a cat in a tree, get children to come up with their own ideas.

Physical skills can also be incorporated into this activity.

Benefits

Can support skills, other areas of learning, topics, imagination, spatial awareness and children reluctant to do physical activities.

Areas of Learning this Activity Covers

* Expressive arts, design and creative development
* Knowledge of and understanding the world
* Language, literacy and communication
* Personal, Social and Emotional Development
* Social, Moral, Spiritual and Cultural Development

THE BOAT (USING MINI YO! OR OTHER YOGA-BASED CARDS)

Sit on the floor with your feet flat on the ground.

Pull stomach in tight and keep back straight.

Put hands on the floor behind your bottom.

Lift feet off the ground (the lower and the straighter your legs the harder it is).

If you can, lift your hands off the floor and hold them straight out in front of you.

Hold the position for a short while.

Pretend you are in a stormy sea and the boat capsizes to the one side.

The boat manages to float back to normal.

It capsizes the other way.

It manages to float back to normal again.

Pretend to row the boat, moving arms back and forth out to the side.

Throw your anchor overboard and dock (put your hands and feet down).

Benefits

This develops balance and core strength, uses imagination and communication.

Areas of Learning this Activity Covers

* Expressive arts, design and creative development
* Knowledge of and understanding the world
* Language, literacy and communication

INDEX